GENERATION EVERYONE!

A Guide to Generational Harmony @ Work, School, & Home

Dillon Knight Kalkhurst

First published in 2018

ISBN-13: 978-1722660420

ISBN-10: 1722660422

Library of Congress Control Number: 2018903003

Printed in the USA

Contents

Dedication

This book is dedicated to my beautiful and supportive wife, Linda, and our awesome son, Jordan.

Linda, you always listen with a smile to my endless ramblings about whatever is flying through my overactive brain. You have supported my every dream, with a hint of much needed "cautious optimism." I appreciate every sacrifice you have made in supporting me and raising our amazing son. You are my best friend and the world's greatest "Gen X-Baby Boomer Cusper" mom.

Jordan, my "iGen-Millennial Cusper" son, you have had to endure my outward personality style and have quietly observed your dad's endless pursuits of the "next big thing." Thank you for allowing me to use you and your friends as a "live-in Millennial-iGen focus group." You have a big heart and you have made me very proud.

I love you both.

Foreword
by Dr. Deborah Gilboa, MD

So, who do you think said the following?...

"The children now love luxury; they have bad manners, contempt for authority; they show disrespect for elders and love chatter in place of exercise. Children are now tyrants, not the servants of their households. They no longer rise when elders enter the room. They contradict their parents, chatter before company, gobble up dainties at the table, cross their legs, and tyrannize their teachers."

When I show this quote and ask audiences this question, I get answers from "Jesus" to "Benjamin Franklin" to "Mister Rogers." The answer goes back 400 years before the writings attributed to Jesus, all the way to Socrates. The idea that it's the next generation who are disrespectful, who disrupt, who ruin everything... it's not new! There have been generational disconnections probably as long as there have been people.

I first met Dillon when he was working at Scholastic, in charge of the engagement, education and motivation of their 1.6 million parent and grandparent volunteers. His knowledge and insight regarding how to connect with people of each generation plumbs the depths while staying grounded in the practical. If you, in your own work, volunteering or family, need to interact intergenerationally, you've picked up the right book.

As a parenting and youth development expert who speaks to middle and high schoolers, college students, military recruits, teachers, coaches, grandparents, university faculty, corporate leaders and Senators, I can tell you – generational disruption is a thing. As a family physician, I know that this "thing" impacts not only how we view each other, but also the very fabric of our families, our health, and our happiness.

Dillon gives you the data – and he delivers it in an engaging way. You'll learn just as much about your own generation as you will learn about any of the others. Did you know that there are currently five generations active in the workforce? Gone are the days of all grandparents living the retiree life. No wonder there are so many situations, from daycare drop off to job interviews and PTA meetings, in which you can see the interaction between generations and how quickly it can get off track.

Dillon gives you the insight into how each generation views the role of work in their lives, as well as their expectations from family, and how they spend their free time. This book also explores what people in each generation value most in their child's education and even why they would choose a particular camp, extra-curricular activity, or vacation spot. Wouldn't you agree that this is incredibly valuable information for business owners, educators, community leaders and event planners?

Finally, and most importantly, Dillon shares his own expertise as well as that of other experts in their respective fields. Their expertise will certainly yield actionable strategies for you. How can you market to each generation? How can you motivate them? How can you lead a group with generational diversity? How can you see the generation disruption that will forever be a part of our society as the strength that it is? After reading this book, you'll have the answers to these questions and many more.

Once you see through the lens offered in this book, you'll find that many, if not all, of your personal and professional interactions will benefit from your newfound wisdom. You will have a new perspective on communication and what success means in each of your relationships. You'll find yourself, as I have, wanting to gift this book to most everyone you know. So, keep this book on the top of your stack – be it on your screen or on your nightstand – and take from it the answers that will seem so obvious once you read them.

Deborah Gilboa, MD

Author of "Get the Behavior You Want… Without Being the Parent You Hate!"

Author's Preface

I am a Baby Boomer. No wait, I am a Generation X'er. Actually, I am what you will learn in this book, a "cusper." A cusper is someone who was born on, or around the year that the prior generation transitions to the next. Those years will vary by about five years depending on who you speak with. Since I was born in 1965, which was an awesome year by the way, I am a *quinquagenarian*. Yes, that is a word for someone who is fifty years of age. It seems there are labels for everything these days, doesn't it?

So far, it has been a great ride, on a personal and professional level. I've had the benefit of working in, and around K-12 education for most of my career. That unique experience gave me tremendous insight into the generations. I've observed little ones enter preschool and followed them through elementary school, secondary school and on to college, where they eventually began their chosen careers and became parents.

I have observed parents from multiple generations and have helped my companies course-correct to meet ever-changing parenting styles. I've observed different generations of teachers and educators and I documented the constant changes in the ways they engage parents and maximize student efficacy.

Finally, I have consulted with hundreds of Fortune 500 companies, school districts, media organizations, foundations, and nonprofits on the most effective way to engage different generations of employees, educators, moms, dads and their children. By engagement, I mean purchasing a product or a brand, recruiting volunteers, communicating with parents, fundraising or aligning employees and associates with the perfect social impact strategy.

I've spent my entire career helping organizations increase employee and customer engagement. Each generation responds in different ways as it relates to customer, employee, parent or community engagement.

Recently, I had the pleasure of managing the volunteer engagement strategy for a large one-hundred-year-old children's book publisher. They relied on parent volunteers, mostly "Millennial Parents" and a good majority of the company leadership were late Gen X'ers and Boomers. I started to see challenges in the way the company and their school clients were communicating with their new generation of employees, customers and parents. With that experience, I became an expert in Millennials, especially Millennial moms and dads. I also learned a lot about the students and the kids, our youngest generation, the iGens.

As I started speaking around the U.S. on the subject, I found that many companies and nonprofits were struggling with "Millennials." Millennials get a bad rap in the media and the workplace, but this is not a one generation challenge. Effective "Intergenerational Communications" is the goal, meaning everyone needs help, first understanding themselves and then understanding their intergenerational counterparts, coworkers and customers.

This is why I wrote this book. I want to share with you everything I have learned. Whether you are from the Silent

Generation, a Baby Boomer, Generation X, Y or Z, you will learn more about yourself and everyone in your life. It is time to embrace our newfound "Age Diversity."

In this book, we will dive deep into each of the five generations that are active in today's economy. It is important that you understand that we are talking in generalities - and I caution you not to assume someone is the way they are simply because of the year they were born. The values and preferences of each generation are generally the same; however, there will be roughly fifteen percent from each generation that will fall outside of their generational cohorts based on out of the ordinary life experiences. We will also discuss the "cuspers," those born around the generational transition years who may have one foot planted in their older generation and the other foot on their younger side. Some are starting to use the new cusper term, "Xennials" to describe those born in the early eighties, signifying they are half Generation X and half Millennial.

We will specifically explore eight different business segments or categories like media and entertainment, parenting, education, food and beverage, real estate, transportation, pet care, and volunteer and philanthropy. We will discuss how the younger and aging generations are disrupting and transforming their industries. To gain additional insight, I interviewed industry experts like…

Deborah Gilboa, MD, aka "Dr. G." Parenting Expert and Keynote Speaker. Author of many books including, "Get the Behavior You Want… Without Being the Parent You Hate!"

Gayle Troberman: Chief Marketing Officer at iHeartMedia.

Maria Bailey: Mom Engagement Expert, Foremost Global Marketing to Moms Expert, Author, Host of Mom Talk Radio, and CEO at BSM Media, Inc.

Carl Venters: Past Vice Chairman of The National Association of Broadcasters

Scott Lohman: VP Business of Sales and Marketing at VolunteerMatch.

Brock Weatherup: EVP Strategic Innovation and Digital Experience, PETCO.

Tom Kersting: Renowned Psychotherapist. Author of the book "Disconnected: How to Reconnect Our Digitally Distracted Kids

By reading this book, you will become self-aware about your own generation and have a general understanding of what motivators influence other generations. My goals are to help you become self-aware, dispel generational stereotypes and embrace "age diversity." Communication is the foundation for a healthy workplace, and a robust sales and marketing plan. GENERATION EVERYONE! will help you embrace and leverage the strengths of EVERYONE in your circle of influence.

Introduction

For the first time in our history, there are five unique generations active in the economy. The Silent Generation, Baby Boomers, Generation X, Generation Y (Millennials) and our youngest, Generation Z, or as I like to call them, iGen.

The world is experiencing communication challenges like no other time before. Companies are having challenges recruiting, inspiring and retaining Millennials. They are also struggling with clear succession plans to replace their aging and soon to retire, leadership teams. Marketers are having to constantly course-correct to engage with the different purchasing habits of each generation. With an ever-growing population of age-diverse parents, schools are finding out that their "old-school" family engagement methods are not connecting with their Millennial parents. Nearly all the new teachers in k-12 schools today are Millennials and they are motivated differently than past generations. Nonprofits are finding the old "donation-based" fundraising models to be falling short. Their stagnant volunteer engagement processes are also failing. They are having to adjust their entire volunteer strategy to meet the needs of an age-diverse volunteer base.

While it is popular these days for some to bash Millennials, and blame them for every challenge, the challenges are much bigger than just Millennials. You will find in this book that I am a big Gen Y fan. I feel Millennials will end up being the most giving generation in our history and the iGens will take it to the next level. I love coaching future Millennial leaders. I spend a great deal of time helping companies engage and embrace their new Millennial talent while, at the same time, educating Millennials on how to become the leaders they aspire to be.

This is an intergenerational challenge. Every generation is unique. They each have their quirks and strengths. **The secret to a thriving workforce, school community or record-breaking sales and revenue is being able to engage effectively across all generations.**

Before we get started, I want to warn you that I may upset you at some point. You may get to the chapter on your generation and say, "that's not me." That's perfectly normal. There is no right or wrong when talking about generational preferences and characteristics. We are talking generalities. For the most part, the preferences and characteristics are spot on, but there will be outliers and you may be one. Understanding the overall generalities will help you become more self-aware and help you understand the general values and motivations of your intergenerational counterparts. While I will refer to data and research in this book, I will also give you my opinions and my general observations, so don't take it personally. With that being said, let's start by looking at how we got to this point.

PART 1

Understanding Each Generation

Chapter 1

A History of Generations

According to the U.S. Census Bureau's latest estimates, there are 7.34 billion people on planet Earth and roughly 326 million people living in the United States as of January 2016.

There are 117 years that separate the youngest and oldest person on Earth. Every second of every day, four new baby earthlings are born. In that same second, two earthlings are returned to dust. It doesn't take a math wizard to see that the world's population is growing and each and every one of us are different and special in our own way.

We all grew up in our own unique surroundings. Our values and personalities were crafted by a variety of different life experiences. Our individual points of view were shaped by our differing life experiences, cultures, ethnicity, gender, and generation. This is what makes our world so interesting and awesome. Our diversity is our greatest strength, yet it is the basis for so many challenges in our home, at work, and across the world.

In case you are wondering, the oldest person on the planet as of this publication lives in Jamaica. That might say something about my favorite laid back place on earth. Yeah mon!

Jamaican born Violet Brown was born 117 years ago. She became the oldest person in the world after the death of Emma Morano, the Italian woman who previously held the title when she died in April 2017. Ms. Emma, who was thought to have been the last surviving person born in the 1800s, was also one of the five oldest people in recorded history, living to be 117 years and 137 days old.

Demography is the study of statistics such as births, deaths, race, income, or the incidence of disease, which illustrate the changing structure of human populations. Don't ask me why, but I have always been fascinated by demography. The demography of the world and the US is changing, especially as it relates to generations. Before we jump into the six living generations, let's play demographer and take a look at some global population rates as it relates to births and deaths. (estimated in 2011)

World Birth and Death Rates

Birth Rate	Death Rate
19 births / 1,000 population	8 deaths / 1,000 population
131.4 million births per year	55.3 million deaths per year
360,000 births per day	151,600 deaths per day
15,000 births each hour	6,316 deaths each hour
250 births each minute	105 deaths each minute
Four births each second of every day	Nearly two deaths each second of every day

According to the National Center for Health Statistics, Today's average life expectancy in the US is approximately 78.7 years. In 1900, the US life expectancy was only 50.6 years. For centuries prior to the 1800s, the worldwide life expectancy was somewhere in the mid-30s, depending on where you lived. While there are many contributing factors that determine life expectancy, there were two game changers.

First was the introduction of Penicillin in the early 1900s. This alone nearly doubled the life expectancy in many areas of the world. The second game changer is the rise of "developing countries." Globalization and the global economy are transforming countries that were very poor in

5

the nineteenth and twentieth centuries into some of the fastest growing middle-class societies on the planet. The rise in middle class brings more resources like education and health care, which increases life expectancy dramatically.

Hundreds of years ago, generations were typically thought of as biological relationships within families, generally male. Grandfathers, fathers, sons, etc. Nobody talked about generations in terms of external groups of "like people" because most people were gone by the time they reached their fortieth birthday.

It was the Europeans that created the idea of generations from the thought that individuals who were born and raised around the same time period shared character building experiences. The French lexicographer Émile Littré defined a generation in 1863 as "*all men living more or less in the same time.*" During that time, there were basically old people and young people, there was no in between. So the term generation was used to differentiate between the older generation and youth. It is a lot more complicated now.

There are now six living generations on earth, with five of them still very active in the economy and in the workplace. This is creating a substantial communication challenge for managers, educators and marketers from every industry.

The boundaries that define generations are not universally agreed upon. You can find a five-year swing one way or another, depending on who you talk to. Regardless of the exact year that a generation changed, the changes carry important implications in business and government. The size, financial security, values, attitudes, and general health of each generation shapes everything from marketing

6

campaigns to insurance and social welfare benefits, as well as workplace engagement and productivity.

For the past 40 years, corporate human resource departments, advertising agencies, school districts and even local, state and federal governments have focused on "diversity." For most of those years, diversity was primarily about ethnicity or gender. Today, we have a new kind of diversity and it is called "Age Diversity."

To their credit, human resource departments have been addressing ageism for some time now. Ageism is prejudice or discrimination based on a person's age. For the most part, ageism concerns were usually centered around company layoffs or promotions. Today, there is no getting around the fact that companies and organizations will require an age-diverse workforce. They will also have to learn to market to an increasingly age diverse customer base that requires entirely different engagement tactics.

Generation	Birth Year and Age of Adults in 2017	US Population
Greatest	Born Before 1927 Age: 90+	3.7M
Silent-Traditionalist	Born 1928-1945 Age: 72-89	28.3M
Baby Boomers	Born 1946-1964 Age: 53-71	75.5M
Generation X Forgotten	Born 1965-1980 Age: 37-52	65.7M
Gen Y Millennials	Born: 1981-1998 Age: 20-36	79.4M
Generation Z iGen	1999-Today Age: 19 and Below	73.6M

The preceding snapshot illustrates how the generations break down in the U.S. according to the Pew Research Center (as of January 2016).

There they are, those Millennials. Last year, Generation Y became the largest generation on the planet.

Millennials also recently became the largest in the workforce as well. As of May 2017, there were 157,700,000 people in the US labor force with 6.8 million or 4.3% unemployed.

Here is a snapshot of how the generations break out in the US labor force according to the Pew Research Center (2015).

Generation	US Labor Force	Approximate % Labor Force
Silent	3.7M	2%
Baby Boomers	44.6M	29%
Generation X Forgotten	52.7M	33%
Gen Y Millennials	53.5M	34%
Generation Z iGen	3.2M	2%

The Baby Boomer generation began retiring over the past decade, and the expectation is that 10,000 Boomers will exit the workforce each day by the end of the 2020s. Because of this mass exodus, it is estimated that Millennials will represent seventy-five percent of the US workforce by the year 2025.

While Millennials are the largest participants in the workforce today, Baby Boomers and Gen X'ers still

8

represent the largest percentage of managers and people in senior leadership roles. In a 2011 survey conducted by Career Builder, nearly one-third of companies with more than 1,000 employees agreed that they don't have a succession planning program in their organization. This is a scary prospect. Who will take the reins when these older leaders retire? That's right, it will be the Millennials.

It will be imperative for companies and organizations to do everything they can to have their Millennial employees trained and ready to lead. Unfortunately, many Millennials lack the soft skills required to be effective leaders in today's sensitive workplace environment.

Chapter 2

The Cuspers

Are you from the Greatest Generation, a Traditionalist, or a Baby Boomer? Are you from the Forgotten Generation, Generation X? Are you Gen Y or a Millennial? How about our youngest generation who some call Generation Z, or as I like to call them, iGen?

There are various names for each of the generations and people have their favorites. No matter what you call a generation, they were generally born around the same time, usually within a 15 to 20-year span. For example, 1965 was the year many demographers put an end to the Baby Boomer generation and introduced the world to Generation X. Anyone born after that year, was now part of a brand-new generation.

Remember, there can be a five-year discrepancy from various sources on what the exact year the generations changed. Some people say Boomers ended as early as 1960, but I like to use the year I was born, 1965.

For those of us born near the generation transition year, things can be a bit confusing - especially when listening to people describe the different generations and their stereotypes. When I look at the typical Baby Boomer and Generation X stereotypes, I clearly feel a connection with both generations. It's like I straddle the line between the generations, acting like a Boomer in one instant and then a Gen Xer the next. This confusion brought about terms like the Straddle Generation, the Sandwich Generation, or as most demographers refer today as, The Cuspers.

A Cusper is simply a term for someone born on the cusp of two different generations. There have been a few ridiculous names thrown around for these Cuspers as well. For example, the generation between Millennials and Gen Xers has been coined the Xennials.

An Xennial could be defined as a micro generation born during the cusp years of Gen Xers and Millennials (between 1977-1983) - when the original Star Wars trilogy was released. Xennials experienced an analog childhood and a digital adulthood (think Mark Zuckerberg). They can possess both Gen X cynicism and Millennial optimism and drive.

If you were born in, say 1981, on the cusp of Generation X and the Millennials, you may have been left out of your older Gen X sibling's grunge-loving style. You probably didn't watch MTV 24-7. On the other hand, when the younger Millennials were toddlers, you were already learning to drive. You may have graduated from college before Facebook, Instagram, Snapchat, and other forms of social media became a way of life. You remember a time when more people had pagers than cell phones and you had to memorize your friend's phone numbers. There can be a stark difference between the youngest and oldest in any generation.

The term Xennial was dubbed by Dan Woodman, an associate professor of Sociology at the University of Melbourne. He was born in 1980. Woodman, like many of us Cuspers, spent much of his life wondering what generation he fit into. "It was a particularly unique experience. You had a childhood, youth and adolescence free of having to worry about social media posts and mobile phones. It was a time when we had to organize to catch up with our friends on the weekends using a landline telephone, and actually pick a time and place and turn up there." he said.

13

Those of us born in the mid-60s were the original Cuspers, sometimes called the "Sandwich Generation." Sandwiched between our free-spirited Boomer parent's generation and the technology-enabled younger generation. I clearly wrestle with this almost daily. Nothing has divided generations more than the rapid ascent of personal technology. For Baby Boomers, there were technological advances, but on a larger scale. They witnessed the space race and saw a man land on the moon. They also experienced TV for the first time in color!

The Internet changed everything, and then, mobile access was like pouring gasoline on the fire that was already raging. Boomer/GenX Cuspers had the biggest learning curve with this exciting new technology and many of us have a love-hate relationship with it and are frustrated by this internal conflict daily.

As a teen, I grew up in a time when there was no internet. If you were bullied at school, you could go home and get away from it. Now, bullies can chase you through the internet and social media after school, through the night and even across state lines. If there was a party I wasn't invited to, I wouldn't know about it while it was happening. Now I can see actual images and Snapchat videos of everyone, but me, having fun. When we were teens, "mobile phone" meant you had a fifty-foot wire that would reach from the landline phone on the kitchen wall down the hall, under your locked bedroom door, to your bed. That was freedom!

Not a day goes by that I don't think about "shutting it down." I clamor for those good old days when I could escape, walk on the beach, play in the woods, and nobody could interrupt my solitude. However, at the same time, I absolutely love

14

having a credit card-sized device in my pocket that can answer any question on earth in less than a second. I experience a constant pull between my quest for Baby Boomer solitude and my Gen X twenty-four-seven connectivity.

It is a common scene across the world today. It seems people can't go 30-seconds without "checking in." The Baby Boomer in me looks at those types of people in disgust, walking around in a daze, heads down in their devices, as the world passes them by. The Gen Xer in me sees those same people and knows they are seeing more of the world in a single glance at their device than we could have seen in a week's worth of the 6:30 evening news. The world is passing by, it is just passing through their mobile devices at the speed of light, and in abbreviated sound bites. Then I revert back and feel sadness for them because I feel mobile phones could bring an end to one of my favorite pastimes: "people watching."

I read a fantastic book recently, *"The End of Absence, Reclaiming What We Have Lost in A World of Constant Connection"* by Michael Harris.

Michael is a journalist and a Boomer/GenX Cusper. Not many industries have been disrupted by the internet and mobile devices more than journalism, so Michael has a really good perspective on how mobile devices have not only changed the world, but also how they have changed the mind.

In his book, Michael notes, "soon enough, nobody will remember life before the internet. What does this unavoidable fact mean? For future generations, it won't

15

mean anything very obvious. They will be so immersed in online life that questions about the internet's basic purpose or meaning will vanish. But those of us who have lived both with and without the crowded connectivity of online life, have a rare opportunity. We can still recognize the difference between 'Before and After.' We catch ourselves idly reaching for our phones at the bus stop. Or we notice how, mid-conversation, a fumbling friend dives into the perfect recall of Google."

In *The End of Absence*, Michael Harris argues that, amid all the changes we're experiencing, the most interesting change is the one that future generations will find hardest to grasp. That is the end of absence—the loss of lack. The daydreaming silences in our lives are filled and the burning solitudes are extinguished. There's no true "free time" when you carry a smartphone. Today's rarest commodity is the chance to be alone with your own thoughts.

People watching is when you observe what is going on all around you. Some people watching locations are better than others. My favorite is South Beach, Miami. In college, at East Carolina University, I loved sitting on the wall in front of the student store between classes and taking it all in.

I am afraid the art of people watching may become a thing of the past. If you don't believe me, take a subway ride. Stand at a bus stop. Look around next time you are in an airport. You will see that nearly everyone is head down, earphones in, tuning out what is near, so that they can be fed what others want them to see.

Absence is a gift. People watching is a form of absence. It offers a lack of certainty. It forces you to wonder. It lets you

16

look at a person and write stories in your mind. I wonder what he does for a living. I wonder where he is coming from and where is he going. When you sit on a beach or alone in your backyard, you have the opportunity to dream, to think about random things that form a basis for creativity. If you constantly pull out that phone, you give up that freedom to dream and are at the mercy of those sending you their "feed."

Now that's the Baby Boomer in me coming out, and it proves my point about Cuspers and our propensity to hop back and forth from our past to the future, like time travelers.

Yes, it can be very confusing being a Cusper, but it can also be a great asset. Cuspers have the unique ability to understand two generations, or about 35-years of coworkers, employees, friends and relatives. Cuspers in the workplace can be great mentors for younger employees. I truly believe that being a Cusper has helped me identify and hone my ability to fully understand all generations and help others do the same. If you are a Cusper, embrace it and help others do the same.

I spent a good part of my formative years as a DJ in dance clubs and on the radio. Music is one of the things that can define a generation. Most people can hear a song from their past and refer to the exact year when that song was playing on the radio, MTV, Walkman, iPod, or YouTube, depending on your generation. I still love music, and at last count, I possessed over 32,000 songs in my library.

I chose to start each generation chapter, with the exception of the Silent Generation, with a passage from a song that may have been in that generation's music collection. For the Silent Generation, I took a quote from the advertising industry, specifically the hit show "Mad Men" as I feel advertising was a defining and disruptive industry for the Silents.

So, let's get started and talk about the oldest generation active in today's economy, the Silent Generation.

Chapter 3

The Silent Generation
Born Between 1928 - 1945

"Everyone else's tobacco is poisonous. Lucky
Strikes'… is toasted."
Don Draper - AMC's Mad Men

Every generation had unique experiences and historic events that occurred in their formative years. I call them "sign posts." Sign posts are the most memorable events that occurred early in a person's life, usually before they turned 18. These sign posts helped shape their Generation and had an undeniable effect on their attitudes, character, and their deepest values. We will begin each generational chapter with their sign posts.

Sign Posts That Shaped the Silent Generation:

- The Great Depression
- World War II
- The Cold War
- McCarthyism
- The beginnings of the Civil Rights Movement
- As children, they were "Seen, but not Heard."

The Silent Generation refers to people who were born between 1928 and 1945. There are several theories as to where the label 'Silent Generation' originated. The children who grew up during this time worked very hard and kept quiet. It was commonly understood that children should be seen and not heard.

Most of the Silent Generation, or Traditionalists, are retirees. They represent the smallest percentage of the workforce today, roughly 2% or about 3.7 million workers. While they may represent the smallest percentage of the workforce, they also represent the largest voting population in the U.S. and control the largest lobbyist group, the AARP.

Many members of this generation grew up during the Great Depression. Because of this experience, they are very frugal with their money. They have a "waste not, want not" mentality and strive for financial security. Their major aspiration was home ownership. Those in The Silent Generation are the wealthiest generation due to their fiscal responsibility and the fact that many of them own their homes outright, with no debt.

The idea of credit was foreign to this generation. When I told my grandfather, a veteran of WWII, that I wanted to buy a new car and finance it, I remember him saying, "If you can't afford it and can't pay cash, you don't need it." Many of their behaviors were based on experiences from the depression and WWII, when it was common to "go without."

Traditionalists were raised in a time of war and uncertainty. Many of the Silent Generation's men served in the military and fought in World War II. Or they were children, growing up while most of the men in their lives were deployed. The women of the Silent Generation typically stayed at home to raise children and, if they worked, their jobs were centered around supporting the troops. Because of their military upbringing, they are very patriotic, and loyal to their country. They understand the nobility of sacrifice for the common good. Many support conservatism and traditional family values.

How Does The Silent Generation Communicate?

Most of the economic advances that occurred in the Silent Generation's formative years centered around manufacturing. The automobile was their signature product. They were the generation that formed labor unions, primarily around manufacturing industries. The Silent Generation is largely disengaged with their attitudes towards

though there are exceptions. Facebook is an
is exception, because it gives them the ability
with their busy, overscheduled children and
en in a visual and more consistent manner.

If you want to communicate with members of the Silent
Generation effectively, you need to pull out a pen and paper
and write them a letter. While their communication
preference is face-to-face, sending a formal letter is always
your best option.

I remember Christmas day vividly when I was growing up.
As soon as we finished opening our gifts, my mom sat us
down with a pen and paper and forced us to hand write thank
you cards to grandma and granddad. We had to write how
we loved their gift, no matter what it was. This is a practice
that I continued until the day they passed. I believe this
practice is a lost art, especially with the advent of email,
texting, and even apps that can send animated "thank you"
notes with dancing puppies and exploding fireworks. Even
with those neat techno-thank yous, I can tell you that my
grandma Dixie, who lived to be 97 years young, would not
have been amused if we had sent her anything less than a
handwritten note, expressing our thanks and love.

The Silent Generation as Customers

Today, you will most likely interact with the Silent
Generation as a customer since many are retired and finally
spending some of their retirement savings. It is important to
understand that, while they may be the wealthiest generation,
they intend to stay that way until they leave us. They still
have that 'waste not, want not' attitude. When they do spend
their money, they put a lot of thought into it.

Traditionalists want to talk to you. They expect attentive and respectful customer service. Forcing the Silent Generation to interact with an endless "press # for ?" system will quickly frustrate them. Even though WWII is over fifty years behind them, Traditionalists are still very dedicated to the USA and will seek out products and services that proudly state, "made in the USA." This generation also responds well to rewards and loyalty programs and expect it for their long-term relationship with your brand or service.

Finally, they appreciate solid, reputable products with history and longevity and do not respond well to changes in what they have been buying for years.

The Silent Generation at Work

When members of the Silent Generation got a job, it was a job for life. The Silent Generation came home from the War, landed a job, worked very hard and expected to stay at that job until their retirement party. Think Mad Men. My how times have changed.

If you have a member of the Silent Generation on your team at work, you are fortunate. They are very loyal to their employers and they expect the same in return. For the most part, they possess superb interpersonal skills, primarily because actually talking to someone was the only way to communicate for most of their lives. Speaking of communication, remember that they prefer the written word, and that goes for the workplace as well. Letters and memos work best for general communication. When it comes to feedback and coaching, one-on-one and in-person meetings are most effective with this generation of worker. When giving feedback and instruction, you should try to be as explicit and detailed as possible.

Unlike their younger cohorts, the Silent Generation expects feedback only when something needs correction. With this generation, no news is good news. Principals and teachers in schools should keep this in mind now that they have multiple generations sharing the parenting responsibilities. Millennial parents expect constant feedback about their child's progress while Grandparent caretakers will become alarmed if they receive a call from the school, automatically assuming something is wrong.

Traditionalists are motivated by a fair rewards system. They value job security, which includes long-term retirement, pensions and 401k programs. They also believe promotions, raises, and recognition should come from job tenure and they expect you to respect their seniority. When it comes to recognition as it relates to productivity, timeliness, work ethic etc., they would rather receive it in private, not drawing attention to it around the office.

Chapter 4

The Baby Boomers
Born Between 1946 - 1964

"You say you want a revolution. Well, you
know we all want to change the world."
Revolution Song – The Beatles

Sign Posts That Shaped Baby Boomers

- Assassinations of JFK, Robert Kennedy, and Martin Luther King, Jr.
- The Cold War
- The Space Race and the Walk on the Moon
- The Vietnam War
- Protests and Sit-ins
- Woodstock
- Civil rights, Women's rights, and Environmental Movements
- Watergate
- Nixon's Resignation
- Self-discovery

The term Baby Boomers, or the Boomers, refer to the generation born during the 'baby boom' following World War II, usually in the period between 1946 and 1964. The term baby boom, refers to a conspicuous rise in childbirth. This term has been common in American English since the late 19th century.

The Baby Boomers grew up in a time with a lot of social change and an uncertain future. Job security was their primary aspiration. Television was their signature product, and the TV brought all the world's injustices right into their living rooms.

For the first time in history, everyday Americans could visually see the horrors of war. Vietnam was the first televised war. Because of this, the Baby Boomer generation started to question the status quo. Where Traditionalists said, "These are the Rules," Boomers said, "Let's Talk About The Rules." They would no longer be silent.

How Do Baby Boomers Communicate?

My company, D. Knight Marketing, Inc. helps organizations maximize their "age diversity." With the majority of our corporate, school and education clients, communication is the number one challenge they face. Most of those communication challenges originate from differences in personality and generational preferences.

In schools for example, a one size fits all parent communication strategy will no longer work. You have young Millennials and Gen Xers as parents and an ever-growing Boomer and Traditionalist parent–base who have had to take over the parenting responsibilities for their grandchildren. To reach parents, teachers should use the communication preference that each parent prefers. As a rule, younger parents respond to mobile-based communication, where older parents require a phone call or handwritten note sent home in the child's backpack. Teachers should ask each of their students' parents how they would like to be contacted on the first day of class and then make note of their preferences through all of their communications throughout the school year.

At work, the Baby Boomers ushered in a less formal style of communication. They were the first generation to use first names at the office, even with their superiors. Boomers prefer to connect by telephone - and I mean with your voice, not your fingers. Have you ever sent a quick question by text to a Baby Boomer and then they immediately call you? Talking to a real human is their preferred style.

The Boomers prefer a more personable and relational communication style as well. Don't just send the facts

27

ma'am. Inject a little of your personality in your communications with Boomers to strengthen the overall relationship. This generation also expects respectful communication and returned calls if they do not initially reach you.

Baby Boomers as Customers

Boomers are not saving money like their Traditionalist parents. In a way, they are rebelling against their stingy parents by attaining a good paying job and spending everything they make. Boomers are the last generation that will benefit from company pensions, unless they are in a government job which, as of today, still provides some form of pension. Many of the Boomers have also benefited from inheritances, trusts, or family businesses left to them by their Traditionalist parents. Unfortunately for the Gen Xers, it doesn't look like that trend is going to continue for them. Boomers will be the first to tell you how hard they have worked and how they fully intend to finish life with a bang. I have a Boomer neighbor who recently retired. He has all the toys, such as a beach house, boats, nice cars and a Harley. His favorite line is "I want to die exhausted."

Baby Boomers are retiring at a rate of 10,000 per day. Marketers are taking note. "Nursing Homes" have been replaced by 55-Plus "Adult Active Lifestyle Communities." One of the most successful examples is The Villages in Central Florida. The Villages offers every activity you could imagine - from a lifetime of free golf to polo.

Their website proudly states… "Be assured that you will find a group in The Villages with the same hobbies and interests that you enjoy. If you have dreamed of someday having time to devote to your special interest, now the world of self-enrichment is at your doorstep. Art, astronomy, clowning, bird watching, collecting, exploring, fishing, genealogy, language, photography, scuba diving, canoeing, and a golf cart drill team are just a few of the groups that are always looking for interested members."

Ok, what the heck is "clowning?" I can't wait to retire and join the golf cart drill team. LOL! This is the real deal. There are golf cars at The Villages that cost more than my 'real' car.

The Villages started 30 years ago and has experienced a 300% population explosion over the past four years. Today, more than 157,000 Boomers and Traditionalists call the Villages home. Boomers and Traditionalists are still the most powerful voting bloc. The Villages is a "must stop" for anyone seeking political office in Florida or the U.S. The success of the Villages has paved the way for a host of upstart 55+ communities seeking to get a piece of the retiring Boomers' hard-earned savings. Baby Boomer icon, Jimmy Buffett, has even thrown his Parrot Head in the ring. He is working with Minto Communities to open Latitude Margaritaville in several locations across the U.S. One of these communities is in Daytona Beach, Florida, not too far from where I live. The community will eventually be home to Boomers and Xers who will be chillin' in 7,000 Key West themed homes. It even includes a Margaritaville oceanfront beach club.

Nobody paints a better image of how Boomers and older Gen Xers want to live than Jimmy Buffett. 70-year-old Buffett still sells out stadiums wherever he tours, sometimes selling out multiple nights at a whopping $276 average ticket price for his top shows. It's been 40 years since he released the Boomer's Retirement Theme Song "Margaritaville." Now you can actually live your Margaritaville retirement dream, at a hefty price tag, I might add. These active adult communities are providing Boomers a way to postpone the inevitable act of growing up.

Latitude's website says "Escape to the place where fun and relaxation meet. Escape to island-inspired living as you grow older, but not up. Escape to Latitude Margaritaville."

It is a sure bet that Boomers will be enticed by Buffett's new community and will be escaping with their well-earned retirement savings and "Wasting away in Margaritaville," sooner than later.

Boomers were the first generation to purchase material things to impress others. Traditionalists were happy in a modest two-bedroom, one bath, ranch style home with a single car garage. After all, what more do you need? Waste not, want not. Boomers, on the other hand, owned multiple cars and built their McMansions.

Have you ever wondered why Americans need a Lexus? Did you know that a Lexus is a Toyota? And Infinity is a Nissan, and Acura is a Honda, etc. I remember visiting Europe in the early 90s and seeing American high-end cars like Lexus and Acura bearing the Toyota and Honda logos. It was the foreign automobile manufacturers that figured out that American Baby Boomers would pay a lot more for a few more bells and whistles - along with that logo. Baby Boomers started the "keeping up with the Joneses" phenomenon, which is a complete 180 from their Traditionalist parents.

30

Baby Boomers at Work

Baby Boomers are known for their extreme loyalty to their employers. They understand the hierarchy and strive to climb the company ladder to get to the next level. They are all about punching the time clock and believe work hours equal productivity. They tend to expect the individuals they manage to work autonomously and work as hard as they do. A forty-hour work week was the minimum requirement. Thus, they tend to be less comfortable in today's collaborative work environments (which attempt to treat all levels of employees as equals when it comes to providing input and feedback). Boomers desperately want respect from younger generations, especially Millennials. In our Intergenerational Engagement work, we find this to be commonplace. Both Millennials and Boomers want respect from each other and, in most cases, they fear they are not getting the respect they deserve. This obviously causes communication issues and dissent in the organization.

Baby Boomers have been working a long time, and they expect to be rewarded for their experience with excellent benefits and respect. Most Boomers are in the later stages of their careers, so saving for retirement is their primary goal. Even the youngest Baby Boomers have passed fifty years of age, so health is becoming a concern. The more health benefits you can provide Boomers, the better.

Leveraging your Boomer employees' experiences is important. While they may not be the most tech-savvy, they can be great leadership role models for younger employees, especially Millennials and iGens. Most established companies have a good number of Baby Boomers in leadership positions, and they are nearing retirement. It is

31

critical that organizations have a clear succession plan. Since many Millennials lack management skills, pairing them with experienced Boomer leaders is ideal for both the employees and the company.

Boomers were the first generation in the workplace to demand personal and professional development. They feel that training contributes to company goals, promotion, and more money. As I mentioned previously, they are usually workaholics and they expect everyone in their organization to work as long and hard as they do. That goes for their kids as well. At the office, they like to have their flock near them, so they can see them "at their desks," working 9-to-5 like Dolly Parton. Many Boomers have a difficult time managing Millennials and the independently wired, Gen Xers who have proven to be highly effective and many times more productive when working remotely. Lack of flexibility, including the opportunity to work remotely, is the leading reason Millennials leave their employers.

The Baby Boomers were also the first generation to expect leadership roles, raises, and career advancement. They were the first generation to prefer public recognition, thus we saw the rise of "Best Seller" trips and annual award galas where employees received recognition in front of their peers for meeting and exceeding company goals.

Finally, salary is still paramount to Boomers. This generation tends to be more traditional than the Millennials, so they still respond well to compensation enhancement opportunities like holiday bonuses, raises and incentives based on performance.

Five Tips for **Managing** Baby Boomers and Traditionalists:

1. Provide professional development, especially around new technology.
2. Ask for their advice and encourage them to share their wisdom.
3. Don't expect them to pull all-nighters like younger employees.
4. Listen to their stories.
5. Use them as mentors for younger employees to help teach soft skills.

Chapter 5

Generation X
Born Between 1965 - 1979

"Now look at them yo-yo's that's the way you
do it. You play the guitar on the MTV.
That ain't workin' that's the way you do it.
Money for nothin' and chicks for free."
Money for Nothing – Dire Straits

Sign Posts That Shaped Generation X

- End of The Vietnam War
- End of the Cold War
- Fall of the Berlin Wall
- AIDS
- MTV
- Microwave Dinners
- Computers
- AOL
- Grunge, Hip-Hop & Rap Music
- Challenger Explosion
- Reaganomics

The term Generation X was originally set out to describe a generation with no identity. Gen X, which was 'often perceived to be disaffected and directionless,' was born in the 'baby bust' period between 1965 and 1979, after the post-war 'baby boom.' This cohort is also significantly smaller than both the Baby Boomers and Generation Y, or the Millennials.

Generation X, The Forgotten Generation, The Slacker Generation, The MTV Generation - whatever you called them, they had the shortest run, roughly 14 years, yet they got the most names. I may be a Boomer/Xer Cusper, but I definitely identify more with Gen X, so I like to claim Gen X as my generation. For this generation, I am allowed to inject my own personal experiences to prove a point or two, so bear with me.

We were called the Forgotten Generation because the Boomers were so profound that by the time they started to fade, the Millennials were here! Now everyone wants to talk about those Millennials. They forgot about us? In many ways, we were forgotten by our parents as well. We were the first generation to really be impacted by divorce and single, working parents. We were the original Latchkey Kids.

Many Gen Xers feel like they got ripped off and have been dealt a bad hand. Marketers never targeted us with their advertising for cool products and services. They went straight from the Boomers to the Millennials.

As you read in the previous generations, the family "hand downs" stopped at Gen X for the most part. Generations before us focused on building wealth and prosperity that they could pass down to their children. Parents of Generation X are expressing clearly that their money is just that, their money, and they intend to spend it on themselves in their "active retirement." I don't have a problem with this. It is their money, and just because you are their children, does not mean that you are entitled to a dime. With that being said, many of my Xer friends and relatives do not feel the same and they often complain about their Boomer parents' lavish and reckless spending.

Like their predecessors, Gen X has no problem working hard, they just added "playing hard" to the equation. We entered careers fully expecting to work our tails off so that, around 65, we would be done and then we can play (like our parents are doing in their 55+ active living communities)!

The problem is, that's not how things are turning out for Generation X. So, some of us feel a bit resentful.

Just when Gen X thought they had their financial ducks in a row, their 401(k) plans were decimated in the great recession and their pensions disappeared. In addition, Gen X is finding it difficult to plan for their financial futures while they're busy paying the day-to-day expenses for everyone in their family. Many Gen X parents are still supporting their Millennial children, and, in some cases, they are also caring for their aging Traditionalists and Baby Boomer parents.

Many Gen Xers are in debt and financially strapped. Of all the past generations, Gen X is the least prepared to retire at this stage of their lives. A study from the Bank of Montreal found that the "sandwich generation" (parents of Millennials and children of Boomers) ages 45 to 65 have only saved an average 30% of what they expect to need for retirement— $291,297 versus their goal of $938,529. That's not too surprising, given that many are still caring both for their kids and now their own parents.

Despite all the unexpected curveballs of life, Gen Xers still enjoy working hard and playing just as hard at the end of the day.

How Does Generation X Communicate?

Generation X communications are largely about relationship building and socializing. Even if the topic of the conversation is serious, a Gen Xer can find a way to lighten the mood.

Unfortunately, Gen Xers prefer email as their primary communications preference. I say unfortunately because, that's me, and if you work with a lot of fellow Gen Xers, it's not uncommon to receive several hundred emails in a given day. Don't even get me started on what happens when you take a week-long vacation. Email is a major source of stress for this generation. Nearly 90% of Gen Xers admit to checking work email while on vacation, primarily because they fear what will be waiting for them when they return.

I remember going to Costa Rica for a week to vacation at a location that was "off the grid." There was no cell service, email, or internet. I was chasing my Baby Boomer solitude and I loved it. Then, I got back to work and found that I had 1,437 unread emails! In one spontaneous response, I highlighted them all and hit "delete." Guess what? Only two people asked me if I got their email. Most of our email is for other people and they are just "keeping us in the loop" or practicing corporate CYA tactics. With that said, it still tops the list as our number one communication preference. Gen Xers are the ones you have a short meeting with and they end the meeting with… "Can you send me that in an email?" Gen X loves their email folders and they use them as an organization tool. They use email to document everything.

Gen X will also communicate through company websites with ease, especially with companies they are doing business with. They tend to prefer website communications for customer service issues. Texting is a comfortable second choice for Gen X and finally, we will pick up the phone and call you as a last resort.

Gen X communication styles are less formal. Humor and a lot of relationship building is usually peppered throughout our messaging. As hard as I have tried, I can't simply send a one-sentence email like my former Baby Boomer Bosses.

Boomers are very comfortable sending an email like this:

Dillon,
Can you send me your weekly sales report by the close of business today???

(no signature or just a capital letter from the person's first name - B)

Where, as a Gen Xer, I might send an email like this to achieve the same result.

Good morning Bill,

I hope you had a fantastic weekend and the family is doing well.

Would it be possible for you send me your weekly sales report by the end of the day? I need to include your report in my meeting with the VP in the morning.

Thanks, and have a productive day.

Cheers,
Dillon

Finally, when communicating with Gen Xers, it is important to use short sound bites. Thanks to technology, Gen X is the generation that fostered the decline in attention spans. While Gen X is not as bad as the Millennials or iGen, they do have a hard time staying focused on long paragraphs or long-winded voice messages. Say what you have to say in short bursts.

Generation X as Customers

Similar to their communication styles, Generation X consumers are all about relationships with companies they do business with. We are the original social butterflies. Remember, we were left alone to fend for ourselves, so we learned early on to communicate in a way that helps us get what we want or need. We can make friends with anyone with ease.

Gen Xers do not respond well to hard selling. Auto dealers, who were once famous for their hard-closing tactics, have had to adjust their sales approaches to a more non-combative relationship-selling style. Now, it's commonplace to visit car lots that have a "no haggle" sales policy. "What you see on the window is the price you pay…Let's talk about how this car is the perfect fit for your family."

In the late 1990s, Gen X consumers forced retailers to start investing in customer research so that they could really understand their primary customer's personality styles. Once retailers fully understood their customer profile, they would invest in hiring the right sales people that could connect or "relate" with their "target customer." They started to invest in training that specifically focused on relationship selling.

Gen X customers will make purchase decisions based as much on the relationship they have developed with the salesperson as the features and benefits. If Gen X doesn't trust a salesperson, they won't buy, no matter how good the product or service is. If they developed a great relationship with the sales associate and eventually decide not to purchase, they can sometimes feel guilty about it.

Generation X was introduced to the internet just about the time they started earning a living. They were the first generation to become comfortable using the internet to research products and price shop, despite the fact that AOL's painfully slow dial-up was the only way to access the internet. Just as they rejected hard sales at the car lot, they also started to question traditional advertising. Just because you see an advertisement for something on TV, doesn't mean it's the best deal or the best option.

My wife is the ultimate Gen X consumer. She will research a dozen different websites and read reviews before she makes a purchase decision. Then she shares her decision with me, I agree, and then she changes her decision again because she found something else in the time it took me to look at her original decision. I love her for this and for many other reasons.

One day my wife came out of the bedroom with a terrible neck ache and said, "That's it…I have to get a new pillow." As a man, I immediately go into "I'll fix this" mode. "I got this!" Everyone who watches any amount of television immediately knows what to buy to solve that problem, right? MY PILLOW!

After all, Mike Lindell personally guarantees that My Pillow will be "The most comfortable pillow she'll ever own" and it's made right here in the U.S.A. If you have read the previous pages, you know that is a perfect pitch to a Silent or Boomer. I would assume that it isn't working as well for the Gen Xers or Millennials. Maybe it is by design since more Boomers and Traditionalists can't sleep through the night?

With a few swipes across her iPhone 7+, also known as her third limb, she instantly found negative reviews of My Pillow on a website called pissedconsumer.com. Who knew there was an entire website dedicated to pissed off consumers? It was probably created by Gen Xers. After reviewing all the options, she landed on an allogeneic bamboo pillow that was about half the price. Now she no longer has neck pain.

The moral of the story? Gen X is not going to believe you just because you say it is so. We are naturally cynical and skeptical.

Another thing we can thank Generation X for is the massive amount of options and choices we have in our everyday shopping experiences. Gen X demanded customization in everything from cars to ketchup. Remember when you would see an advertisement for a car and when you got to the dealership, the price was the same? That is because a car was a car and there were very little differences in models and very few "options" or choices beyond what color you wanted.

I once saw an ad for a BMW 5 Series that I could lease for $399 per month. Wow! I can drive a Beemer for less than $400 a month? I went to the dealership and they laughed about the ad. They told me they could get that car, but they would have to order it. Adding all the "options" or choices that I wanted added $14,000 to the bottom line and skyrocketed my "affordable" monthly lease payment closer to $700! Needless to say, I didn't lease the Beemer.

How about Ketchup? When I was a kid, there was ketchup and there was mustard. Have you looked at the condiment aisle in your local grocery store lately? I recently visited our local Publix grocery store and counted 49 different ketchup choices. The variety included: different brands, different sizes, plastic or glass, fancy, natural, organic, gluten free, sugar free, and high fructose corn syrup free. We have 'choice overload' in our society, and some research has shown this overwhelming choice is a contributing factor to the rise of anxiety in America. Really? Thanks Gen X. We will talk more about anxiety in future chapters.

Let's talk about Gen X food choices. I believe that Gen X demands a diverse selection of food choices because we were deprived of food choices growing up. While Millennials demand and enjoy their "free" choices like free range, cage free, gluten free, etc. Generation X grew up eating anything that was "parent free."

Thanks to the invention of the microwave and our single working parents, we missed a lot of those home cooked meals like June cooked for Ward, Wally and the Beav. We were treated to anything that could be zapped in a minute with little or no parental involvement, and we didn't seem to care at the time. We were independent, empowered, and we enjoyed the quick dinners so we could get back outside and play.

My favorite microwave delicacy was SpaghettiO's. I used to tell my mom that Grandma made better SpaghettiO's than she did, and she would go nuts. Remember those hot dogs with the cheese already stuffed inside? What a mess those things would make when they exploded in the microwave. "Mom, I thought you said 10 minutes!" Speaking of the microwave... how many of you Gen Xers remember your mom yelling at you for standing too close to the microwave for fear that you would get radiation poisoning? Just to clarify, it was ok to shoot radiation into your cheese-stuffed hot dog that you would consume, as long as you didn't watch it too closely.

From a shopping standpoint, Gen Xers are willing to wait "a little" for their product to be delivered. Unlike the Millennials and iGens who were raised in a world of "instant gratification," Gen Xers can wait a day or two to get exactly what they want.

As a lifelong photographer, I had my own dark room as a teen. Talk about an exercise in patience. Imagine this, Millennials. I would load my camera with a roll of film that gave me just 24 opportunities to take the perfect picture. You really had to think about the picture before you snapped it. I would take a picture and I would have no idea how it came out. It was hidden deep inside my camera. I drove home, went into my dark room, mixed the chemicals, took the roll of film out of the camera and exposed the film strip. All in the dark with a dim black light.

After the film strip dried, I would load the picture "negative" into a giant projector and shoot light through it onto a fairly expensive piece of 8 x11 photo paper. Then I would transfer the photo paper to the first of three tubs of toxic chemicals. I would eagerly watch in the dark, black-lit room while the image slowly started to appear. Then I transferred it to the second tray of chemicals. I would then hang the exposed photo paper on a wire with a clothespin to dry before I was able to turn on a light and truly see how the picture turned out. After that tedious process, I would do the same for each of the other 23 pictures.

45

I will never forget when the first 1-hour photo opened in our town. That was unbelievable! So, we Gen Xers have been trained to wait a little for the right outcome. Today, everyone is a photographer and has on average 1,327 pictures in their smartphones. Everyone now has a good camera and the darkroom in the palm of their hands.

Generation X at Work

As I mentioned, Gen X'ers were the latchkey kids. The first generation to grow up in divorced families, forcing mom and/or dad to work outside the home. Their environment caused them to become very self-reliant. They learned how to fend for themselves. This independent upbringing has everything to do with their independent mindset in the workplace today.

Because we had a lot of time to explore and create with little supervision, Gen Xers are good problem solvers. Think about this... when we were teens, we had the opportunity to come home from school, break things, and then we had three to four hours before mom or dad came home to figure out how to fix it. If you couldn't come up with a solution in time, all Hell would fall upon you. That's motivation.

Gen X employees will question authority much more so than their predecessors. Gen X employees were the first to demand "work-life-balance." Because Gen Xers saw both of their Boomer parents work themselves to death for their Traditionalists bosses, many will put their personal lives ahead of their jobs without thinking about it.

Generation X'ers are very flexible and handle change well. This generation is appreciative to have a "job" because many

46

were affected by the Great Recession, thus they are known as dependable and reliable workers that require less direct management. For the most part, Gen Xers hate to be micromanaged. They will perform best when clear goals are set and you let them run.

Many Gen Xers are super creative as well and they will tend to lose focus if clear handrails are not established. Their innate creativity should be encouraged, and they should be brought into situations to help the organization find creative solutions to challenges.

Gen X is the first generation that will not benefit from widespread company pensions. Therefore, the most valued benefit for Gen X is a 401(k) with matching contributions. Only 33% of this generation is on track to have enough savings to retire, so they plan on continuing to work beyond the Baby Boomer's retirement age. Cash is king for Gen X as they seek ways to boost their retirement savings. They expect a competitive salary, and they want to have a clear path to develop and grow their compensation over the next decade. If you do not provide this clear direction, they will leave and find it elsewhere.

In research conducted by the Center for Talent Innovation (CTI), they identified a few thoughts on how organizations can make sure they engage and retain their Generation X employees.

Give Them New Challenges: Gen Xers like to be assigned to new projects that give them the opportunity to work independently. The research from CTI found that nearly three-quarters of Gen Xers (70%) prefer to work independently. Gen Xers are great self-starters. They are individual players who work well in situations where conditions are not well defined. Gen Xers thrive when placed in charge of high-visibility projects that position them in a way that spotlights their abilities throughout the organization.

Encourage Intrapreneurship: Intrapreneurship is when a company encourages employees to create new business opportunities within the current organization. It can also be used to encourage new ways of doing things better that save the company money or increase productivity. Intrapreneurship should be encouraged, especially for Gen X and Millennial employees because it rewards creativity that ultimately helps the business grow.

Gen Xers by nature are entrepreneurial. This has a lot to do with their natural independence and creativity. Organizations should encourage their Gen X employees' entrepreneurial instincts. Following in the footsteps of fellow Gen Xers like Dell computer founder Michael Dell, and Sara Blakely, who created the multimillion-dollar Spanx empire, nearly 39% of Gen X men and 28% of Gen X women aspire to be an entrepreneur. Forward-thinking organizations will encourage their Gen Xers and all their employees to test their wings with company-sponsored ventures rather than have them start their own business elsewhere.

As a Gen Xer, I have always possessed an entrepreneurial spirit. I started my marketing firm when I was in my 20s. Interestingly enough, I enthusiastically thrived in corporate America for more than two decades, primarily because I was given "Intrapreneurship" opportunities within those organizations. The companies I worked for created new positions that allowed me the independence and flexibility

48

to create unique programs that drove incremental revenue from nontraditional sources like sponsorships.

Giving Intrapreneurship-based projects to creative, independent employees will keep them engaged, challenged, and inspired (which will help the company improve employee morale and retention).

It is important to note that while I was experiencing grand success in corporate America, I always had my marketing business in the background, working on it nights and weekends. It never affected my corporate gig and it offered me the opportunity to generate additional income for my family from my creative passions, like photography and videography. After a fun and sometimes challenging ride in corporate America, I eventually relaunched my company as a full service Intergenerational Engagement marketing and consulting firm 25 years later - and I didn't miss a beat.

There are many examples of organizations that are building entrepreneurship into their corporate culture. That's a very smart strategy, considering that as many as 80% of the workforce may be freelancing by the year 2025. Companies like Google and DreamWorks, for example, have formal processes that encourage employees to start and pitch their own businesses to the organization. There have been multiple instances where the companies end up investing in their employees' "side gigs" and, in some cases, eventually acquiring them all together.

Offer and Encourage Flexibility: In order to appeal to Gen X and also Millennial employees, it is important that companies offer flexibility. Extreme jobs, characterized by workweeks of 60-plus hours, unpredictable workloads, tight deadlines, and 24/7 availability are the norm for Gen X. Nearly a third (31%) of Xers make over $75,000 a year slogging through schedules that never stop. Flexible work arrangements, including reduced schedules and virtual workspaces, are checked off as "very important" for 66% of Gen X women and, significantly, 55% of Gen X men. Even childless employees yearn for better work-life balance to pursue their own interests.

Like Baby Boomers, Gen X is also concerned about job security; however, they want to be able to find a job that provides them with some hint of a work-life balance. To feed this need, Gen Xers appreciate paid vacation, sick days, and the aforementioned flexible work schedule (which could include working virtually for some percentage of their work week).

Tips to Managing Gen Xers

In summary, Generation X employees are hardworking, responsible and resourceful. They coined the phrase "self-starter."

Here are ten tips to help you successfully engage, motivate, and manage your Gen X team members.
1. Give them work experiences that are challenging and exciting.
2. Show them opportunities to grow, both personally and professionally.
3. Provide them the training and resources to do their job.
4. Treat them like peers, not subordinates.
5. Be very clear with expectations and results and let them run with it.

6. Get rid of silly or obsolete rules.
7. Focus on their families and provide flexible work schedules with virtual work options.
8. Provide individual recognition.
9. Provide constructive feedback often and to the point. They take feedback well and are willing to change quickly if need be.
10. Lighten up and have fun!

Chapter 6

Generation Y - The Millennials
Born Between 1980 - 1995

"You better lose yourself in the music, the moment. You own it, you better never let it go. You only get one shot, do not miss your chance to blow. This opportunity comes once in a lifetime you better."

Lose Yourself– Eminem

Sign Posts That Shaped Generation Y – The Millennials

- Rise of the Internet
- First Laptop
- CDs and DVDs
- Columbine Shooting
- Oklahoma City Bombing
- Waco Massacre
- Y2K
- September 11th
- Terrorism & The War on Terror
- OJ Simpson Trial
- Exxon Valdez Oil Spill
- The Introduction of Social Media

I've been waiting for this chapter and I bet you have as well. What's up with those Millennials? Most of the initial calls from my clients originate from a Boomer or Gen X manager who can't "figure out" Millennials. How do we recruit them? How do we inspire them? How do we retain them? How do we get them to love and buy our products or services?

As I mentioned in the introduction, I have a penchant for Millennials and iGens. I had the pleasure of managing a volunteer program for a major children's publisher that relied on over a million Millennial parents to run their programs in 60,000 schools across the U.S. and, as you know, I have one of those Millennial/iGen Cuspers still living under my roof. He and his friends have been my live-in focus group for nearly two decades.

I like to write in airplanes. When I'm at home, I will head to the library to do most of my writing and blogging. They have these cool phone booth-sized study rooms that help me focus and avoid distractions. To make sure I was in the right "Frame of Mind" to share my thoughts on Millennials, I decided to write this chapter from the belly of the beast. A place where the Millennials congregate and spend most of their time, the 'Gourmet Coffee Cafe.'

So here I sit, eating a cinnamon bagel, sipping on my half-calf, sugar-free, café latte macchiato coffee in the middle of the day at Gold Leaf Coffee Co. in Ormond Beach, Florida. Gold Leaf is owned by Megan, a Millennia/Xer Cusper who proudly identifies herself more with the Millennials, her clientele. Gold Leaf shares space with an eclectic art studio called, Frame of Mind, owned by Victoria, another Millennial. I'm surrounded by super cool Millennials with their tattoos, body piercings, facial hair, sandals and Apple laptops covered with stickers from all the adventures they have experienced. Thanks Megan for letting me lurk in a corner all day, banging away on my Apple laptop (with no stickers). I'm in the zone!

Ok, before you think this chapter is going to be a Millennial bashing session, think again. I sarcastically used some of the well-known Millennial stereotypes in the previous paragraph to highlight some the ridiculousness of this obsession the media and society has in general with Millennials. By the end of this chapter, you are going to find that I believe the Millennial Generation will end up being the most caring, creative and productive generation ever. They are going to leave this world in a better condition than they inherited it.

Currently, the world does have an obsession with Millennials. As a generational researcher, I have a Google Alert set for each generation. For those of you not familiar

55

with Google Alerts, it is a researcher's dream tool. You can set parameters and key words around subjects you are interested in and Google scans the World Wide Web daily for articles from around the world about your exact interest.

Every morning when I wake at 5:00am, I read my alerts before I head to the gym to work on "maintaining" my youthful body, along with a few dozen other Boomer and Gen X "maintainers." I will usually receive anywhere from 5-to-10 alerts about Boomers or Gen Xers and a little more lately about Generation Z, or what I like to call iGen. Millennial alerts are pages and pages long, at least fifty per day. Everyone has something to say about Millennials and a lot of it is just plain crap.

The term for this generation was originally Generation Y. Why? Because it comes after X. How creative. In an alphabetically sensible move, the generation following Generation X should be called Generation Y, right?

What we have learned over the years is that new generations typically don't want to be associated in any way to the previous generation. Gen X was originally called the Baby Busters or Post Boomers. Obviously, we rebelled about that because we did not want to be connected to those "Boomers." So that's how we Gen Xers ended up without an identity, thus we were branded Generation "X."

So where did the term Millennial originate? The term Millennial, referring to the generation entering adulthood around the turn of the 21st century, has been around since the early 1990s. It dates from the 1991 book *Generations* by William Strauss and Neil Howe, which covers their theory of social generations, now known as the

'Strauss-Howe generational theory.' Strauss and Howe have gone on to write several books about the social impact of the Millennials. Additionally, like other generational change years, there is some vagueness as to whether Millennial refers to those entering adulthood around the year 2000, or a few years earlier.

Let's Talk About Stereotypes

Every generation in history originally thinks the generation after them are a bunch of idiots and slackers. Traditionalists called the Baby Boomers potheads and hippies. The Boomers called Gen Xers cynical, disengaged slackers. Now all three of the older generations are having a field day hammering the Millennials. No generation in history has been stereotyped more than Gen Y. Stop me if you've heard some of these. Millennials are entitled, lazy, coddled, selfish, easily offended, sensitive, and not loyal. They hang out in coffee shops, eat gluten free, think they can save the world, and are all living in their parents' basements. It's all about "passion before paycheck."

Millennials have even been accused of killing nearly everything past generations proudly built. Even though I am not a Millennial, I understand why they get upset with all the nonsensical stereotypes and generalities that pundits spew about "their kind."

I follow a lot of Millennial writers and bloggers and one of my favorites is Chloe Bryan. Chloe, a Millennial and Web Culture Reporter at Mashable, has identified 70 things that the media has accused her generation of killing. In her list of murdered products, services and customs, Chloe linked each of them to the actual online article describing the Millennial killing. If you Google *"Chloe Bryan-RIP-Here Are 70 Things Millennials Have Killed"*, you can find her article and read about all those Millennial inspired deaths.

According to Chloe and many of her Millennial cohorts, they've been accused of killing Beer, J. Crew, Department Stores, Motorcycles, Diamonds, Golf, Bar Soap, College Football, Lunch, McDonald's, Vacations, Napkins, Cars, Crowdfunding, Wine, Wine Corks, The Toyota Scion, Fabric Softener, Marriage, The McWrap, Handshakes, The Canadian Tourism Industry, Light Yogurt, Gambling, Hotels, Relationships, Marmalade, Running, Cereal, The Anti-Aging Industry, Buffalo Wild Wings, Focus Groups, Travel Marketing, Working, Credit, Trees, The American Dream, America, Democracy in General, Home Depot, Self-Pity, The 2016 Presidential Election, Consumerism, Suits, Dinner Dates, Movies, Sex, Gyms, Serendipity, Loyalty Programs, Loyalty in General, Taking Risks, Patriotism, Cruises, Applebee's, Fashion, Hangout Sitcoms, The Big Mac, Stilettos, Romance, The 9-to-5 Workday, The NFL, Gen Xer's Retirement, The Olympics, Brunch, The European Union, Baby Names, Banks, Oil, Everything!

What a list! As I said, there really is news or a blog post about every one of these. Check it out.

It is way past the time to stop this stereotyping nonsense and highlight the positive influences that each generation can bring to the workplace and the world.

While no one can deny there are plenty of Millennial stereotypes, Millennials and their younger cohorts also throw around stereotypes about Gen Xers and Boomers alike. Stereotypes go both ways and, for the most part, they

58

are damaging. I've heard many a Millennial fire off a few of their own stereotypes about their older coworkers. "Boomers and Gen Xers don't get technology, they are all just waiting to retire, or they are jealous that they aren't having fun like us." (Megan just told me that one over my shoulder). Granted, there are some truths embedded in these stereotypes, but you cannot use them to accurately describe an entire generation.

I started this chapter with some of these stereotypes to make a point, and yes, I am still sitting in Megan's coffee shop four hours later and I am still surrounded by super cool Millennials with their tattoos, body piercings, facial hair, sandals, and laptops covered with stickers from all the adventures they have experienced. So what!

For the first time in our history, we have five generations active in the economy. For the first time, companies, schools, and nonprofit organizations have been given the gift of "age diversity." Each generation was awesome in their own way and they have a lot to share with their intergenerational counterparts. Where one generation may have been weak in a particular area, that area is typically another generation's strength. This goes for the young and the old or "experienced." Again, I am not denying that there isn't some truth to those stereotypes because, if that stuff wasn't happening, the stereotype would never have been established. Take it with a grain of salt.

For workplaces to embrace and grow from their age diversity, step one is to **REMOVE ALL STEREOTYPES** and encourage everyone to learn from each other.

59

Age Diversity provides a built-in mentoring program. I'll use one example to prove my point. Yes, it is true that some Boomers may be a little tech challenged. And it is true that some Millennials may lack some soft skills that are required for them to become great leaders. Chances are, your Millennial employee is tech savvy and your Boomer employee has had many years practicing soft skills that have helped them climb the company ladder. There it is, instant co-mentorship in your organization. Pair them up and challenge them to learn something new.

There are already examples around the world where the age diversity benefit is becoming a real business model. Residential leasing companies have started to promote "Boom Mates." Millennials who, early in their careers, are finding it difficult to afford the rising costs of apartment rentals where they need to live to be close to their jobs. At the same time, Baby Boomers and other older Americans are wanting to stay in their homes despite rising costs of taxes, insurance, maintenance and other expenses of home ownership.

In a report released by real estate matchmaker, Trulia, nine out of ten Baby Boomers want to stay in their homes even if costs rise. Meanwhile, Millennials are struggling with high housing prices and rent, especially in strong tech centers where many Millennials want to work like Silicon Valley, Seattle, and Boston. In those tech hubs, more housing units or rooms would provide Millennial workers a significant amount of relief from the high rent costs. Fortunately, Baby Boomers with spare rooms, known as "boom-mates," are playing a role in adding more open units to the market.

According to the Trulia report, tens of thousands of homes in the U.S. have nearly 3.6 million unoccupied rooms that could be rented out. Retired and soon-to-be-retired Baby Boomers can make as much as an additional $14,000 a year, simply by renting out a spare room in their home. For Millennials, the option of living with a "boom-mate" as opposed to a one-bedroom apartment could save them $24,000 annually, the report states.

In addition to financial gains, the study also found other benefits to these intergenerational household arrangements. While the boom-mate trend hasn't quite hit the U.S., it has become quite popular in Europe, according to the report. For Boomers, increased social interaction with their Millennial roommates can help fight dementia and regulate blood pressure. It can also eliminate feelings of loneliness, which has been linked to an increased mortality rate. Millennials benefit as well. Boomers can provide guidance and wisdom to a younger roommate while, in exchange, Boomers can learn new technologies, ideas and perspectives. Age diversity is a real win-win!

The Product of Helicopter Parents

As in past generations, the historical sign posts, and the way generations were raised as children in their formative years, followed them into adulthood. In some ways, the children will embrace some of their parent's parenting styles, while in other ways, they completely rebel and want to raise their children completely different.

For example, Boomers grew up in a time where dad worked long hours while mom stayed home and raised the children. It was the 'Leave it to Beaver' era. When those Boomers became parents, the women's liberation movement propelled women and moms to pave their own way. Moms would no longer stay in dysfunctional marriages, which caused divorce rates to skyrocket. Boomer parents were hyper-career focused to the point that some have described them as the original "Me Generation." Moms were now working those long hours as well. This was how the Latchkey Kids came about. The Latchkey Kids, as you learned earlier, are the Gen X kids, and to be fair, some of the younger Baby Boomers were also affected by this phenomenon in their formative teen years.

Gen X kids were largely ignored growing up and were left to fend for themselves. Note to Mom – I love you and I am not accusing you of ignoring us. You did everything you could to raise us with the cards you were dealt. I am sure that was the case with most parents of the Gen X Generation. I'm just saying, not many parents spent time shuttling their kids around to after school activities.

With many societal trends, the pendulum tends to swing from one extreme to the other, spending little time in the middle, or what I refer to, the land of "common sense." We like to over-compensate, over-correct.

When Generation X became parents, they did a complete 180 from their childhood and decided they would not let their kids grow up unsupervised, or unsupported in any way. Granted, societal and environmental changes had something to do with this. In most areas, it seems that it was much safer walking home from school alone as a kid than it is today. At least, that is how it appears. Crime statistics have actually improved over the past thirty years, but perception is reality.

Gen X parents were the first to experience the 24-hour news cycle on television, radio, social media and the internet. When Gen Xers were growing up, there was about two and a half hours of local news broadcasted during the day on a whopping three channels. Today, there is an average of seven local television stations in every city, covering local news in each one. Each of them average eight hours of news coverage per day. Most cities don't have enough news to fill that amount of time, so everything that is remotely negative is covered ad nauseam.

Don Henley was ahead of his time with his hit song, *Dirty Laundry*, that was released in 1982.

"I make my living off the evening news
Just give me something-something I can use
People love it when you lose,
They love dirty laundry

Well, I coulda been an actor, but I wound up here
I just have to look good, I don't have to be clear
Come and whisper in my ear
Give us dirty laundry

Kick 'em when they're up
Kick 'em when they're down"

Henley sang those lines 25 years ago and they ring truer today than ever. Would you agree?

When you watch your local news, it seems that a considerable portion of the news stories originate in neighborhoods that are nowhere near where your children would be playing. Add in the 24-hour national news

63

networks, featuring all the evil worldwide, and the result is terrified parents who would never let their kids venture out alone in our dangerous world.

Gen X and young Boomer parents could not risk having their children wander aimlessly around the neighborhood after school with child molesters, murderers and terrorists lurking around every corner. They couldn't let them run in the woods. They may get lost or hurt.

Gen X parents were working 9-to-5 so what did they do with the chillins after school? They filled their schedules. Enter the overscheduled Millennial child. Constantly being shuttled from one practice to the next. Spending hours on homework each night. Weekends were also scheduled with ball games, scouting, or birthday parties. It was the "End of Absence."

Another major game changer happened as Millennials were in their formative years... and that was the self-esteem movement. In 1969, Nathaniel Branden published "The Psychology of Self-Esteem." Branden insisted that self-esteem was the single most important characteristic a person could possess. This was a time when Gen Xers were kids, but their parents didn't put much thought into how their kids felt about themselves. By default, and probably not intentionally, Gen X kids were allowed to fail, and fail we did. We fell off the tree house and broke an arm. Guess what? Won't do that again. We didn't study for the test and got a big fat "F." Won't do that again. Failure is the ultimate teacher. Once the self-esteem movement was in full swing, failure was to be avoided at all cost.

Parents of the Millennials became fully aware that failure could damage their child's self-esteem. Anything potentially damaging to their kids' self-esteem was eliminated at all costs. Competition was bad and "not fair!" In competitions, someone has to lose and that was unacceptable. Soccer coaches stopped counting goals and handed out trophies to everyone. Teachers threw out their red pencils. Criticism was replaced with ubiquitous, even undeserved, praise. Thus, the advent of the helicopter parent.

I will be the first to admit that my wife and I are good examples of Gen X helicopter parents, although we don't think we were as bad as some of our friends. Helicopter parents got the name because they hovered over their children, just close enough to be able to swoop in whenever their children got too close to the fire or (failure). We wanted to be more like "best friends" to our kids rather than parents.

We asked our children's opinions on everyday household purchases, and marketers took note. Today, children are a central component of nearly every major family decision, even at a very young age. In order to please their children, Gen X parents will take their child's feedback into account on everything from dining out to family vacations to what kind of car to buy. If you don't believe me, pay close attention to the commercials that run on popular children's television networks like Nickelodeon and Cartoon Network. Automobile marketers use children in their ads to entice the kids to go to mom and dad and say "I want that car!" Instead of featuring options that make the car a better machine, like the engine, horsepower, drivetrain, etc, they focus their messaging on the flat screens and entertainment options.

65

Advertisers are also very good at playing to the helicopter mom's desire to be loved and accepted by their kids. Many ads feature moms coming home with a particular product to be greeted with a big hug and kiss from their children because she brought that product home. A Gen X parent thinks, "If I buy that, it will make my child happy." Marketers play to mom's fear as well by honing in on safety features that will protect her child from danger. Don't get offended. Advertisers have been effectively doing this to us since the Mad Men days. It's classic marketing 101.

Many of the Millennials received amazing attention from their parents growing up. Sometimes, not by choice. For example, when our son was in primary school, the school district was forced to do some cost cutting like so many school districts across the country. One of the ways they cut costs was to extend the distance a child could be picked up by a school bus and, unfortunately, we were just under that line.

The assumption was that kids living under four miles should be able to walk or ride their bikes to schools. It wasn't as bad as my traditionalist grandfather, who proudly proclaimed he "walked ten miles to school in the rain and snow, and it was uphill both ways." It was bad and completely unacceptable to assume he could safely make it to and from school. He would have to cross five major intersections and walk a mile beside a six-lane super busy road. That forced my wife to completely alter her lifestyle until our son could drive himself, because someone had to get him to school. The same goes for soccer practice. If you were lucky, you even got delegated to shuttle teammates around as well, because other parents worked and may not have had the flexibility from their employers to do it themselves.

66

As children, Millennial kids were told that they deserved the best and that they could grow up to be anything they wanted to be. They were applauded for every accomplishment. That's right, everyone got a trophy. Older generations understood that there were always winners and losers in life and that you need to do the work and the practice it takes to win. My dad would proudly tell me after losing the championship basketball game, "Second place is last!" Ok, that is a bit harsh, but it is a reality that many Xers and Boomers grew up in. I can also tell you that my dad never came to me when I was ten years old and asked me what kind of car he should buy. He just came home with a new car (with no seatbelts).

We recently downsized from a fairly large home where we raised our son until he was out of high school. It is amazing how much junk you can accumulate over two decades in the same house. I was amazed at the number of trophies we found in our son's closet, the attic, etc.

I remember when he was about 4-years old and he was in karate, which I highly recommend as it does teach discipline and focus (which is critical for a four-year-old). We traveled to a karate tournament. They had him in his little karate outfit, called a "gi," stand at attention in front of a judge. The judge or "sensei" held a thin plastic pre-broken board in front of my son. My tiny son took a bow and kicked the already broken board in half! Everyone erupted in applause and he was handed a trophy with the little gold kicking karate dude on top. He was also promoted to the next color belt. What an incredible boost to his self-esteem.

As parents, did we give our Millennials too many pre-broken boards and cheer when they did something that took little effort? Maybe.

I believe true self-esteem comes from being knocked down, learning from it, and getting back up and doing it right. We let the pendulum swing too far. I am afraid we didn't let the Millennials fail enough to learn valuable life lessons on their own. We spent so much time giving them a competitive advantage, we forgot to let them do the heavy lifting.

Did we mess up as parents? No. Quite the contrary. I truly believe that every generation of parenting did the best that they could to raise great kids. Gen X parents did succeed in raising great Millennial kids, and they love us for it. The Millennial generation was the first to rebel against the "my parents are fools" mindset that older generations had. As kids, the Millennials and iGens as well, actually liked doing things as a family. That's right, they will walk with you at the mall.

Having a "cool parent" is a big deal. This family attachment is following them into pre-adulthood. That is one of the reasons Millennials are not packing their bags on their 18th birthdays like a lot of the Gen X and Boomers did. To be fair, most of their parents don't want them to leave home, even though they will joke about it with all their friends. I remember my 21st birthday. I wanted to go to Vegas. Anywhere that I could do some serious legal "adulting." My son turns 21 soon and just informed me that he would like us to rent a cabin in the Georgia mountains as a family for his birthday. Could it be that one of the drivers for his decision is that he is wanting to disengage from social media and enjoy some nature, some "absence?" I am starting to see a trend with Millennials and iGens as well. When Millennials finally venture out on their own and can make decisions for themselves, many tend to be less scheduled, looking into tiny houses, craving experiences, nature and simpler lifestyles.

Maybe we are best friends. We were good parents, we did what we felt was the right thing to do for our Millennial children. We protected them, gave them every advantage that we may have not received from our parents. Now it's their turn. They'll be okay, and they will be awesome!

How Do Millennial Communicate?

No surprise here, the communications preference for the Millennial generation is texting. A close second is messaging apps and social networking. It looks like email is starting to show up with Millennials, most likely because many of them are now working for Gen X led companies who live and die by the email.

Technology is king for Millennial communication and most of it is mobile. Not all Millennials are digital natives. The oldest Millennials may be able to remember a time when technology was not as sleek and cool. They may remember older forms of technology like earlier cell phones that did not text, but the youngest Millennials, like my son, can't remember life without the internet.

Millennials are also very visually oriented. Video and images work very well and have proven to be more effective in all forms of advertising to Millennials. This is why you see social and messaging apps like Snapchat and Instagram growing at a much faster pace than others. Many Millennials are turning away from Facebook. They still have active

Facebook accounts and check them regularly, but their consistent communications with friends are happening through Instagram and Snapchat.

Millennials are masters of online and mobile communications; however, they may not be as comfortable in face-to face communications. This may explain why Millennials do very well in virtual working arrangements. They also don't care for phone conversations and many rarely check their voicemails. My son, for example, has never set up his voicemail on his iPhone. This makes no sense to me, but it is the Millennial and iGen norm.

Twenty-five percent of Millennials spend five hours per day on their smartphones and 37% look at their phone more than 100 times per day. To communicate with Millennials, you can no longer have a "mobile first" strategy, you need a "mobile only" strategy. If they are not on their mobile devices, chances are they are engaging another screen and in many cases, all at the same time. This "skill" has helped Millennials become masters at multitasking. It is completely natural for a Millennial to be watching TV, checking their social media, and sending a text simultaneously, without missing any of the communications.

When communicating with Millennials, it is important that you try to utilize the methods of communication they prefer the most. Years ago, it would seem inappropriate to try to schedule a business meeting through text, now it is the most effective way.

Communication with Millennials should be short and get to the point. Thanks to advances in technology, Millennials have an even shorter attention span than the Gen Xers. A comScore study pegged the Millennial attention span at about 12 seconds. As a point of reference, a goldfish can focus for about 9 seconds. With lightning fast broadband and faster and faster smartphones, we are all being programmed for instant access and that is abbreviating our attention spans across all generations. When we want to know something, we pick up our phone, open Google, and ask a question. In .041 seconds, you get 76.3 million responses. Today, you don't even have to pick up your phone, just ask Siri or Alexa. Expect that twelve second Millennial attention span to get even shorter for the next generation who has never been without a smartphone in their life.

Millennials as Consumers

Millennials are targeted more than any other generation by marketers and advertisers. This is nothing new. The 18-to-34-year-old demographic has been the bread and butter of most companies for decades. It just so happens that Millennials are in that sweet spot right now. If you are an older Gen Xer or a Boomer, you may feel like advertisers are not talking to you, and you are right. Unless you are tuned into a channel or program that is targeted toward an older demographic, you may feel like everyone in the ads looks like your kids.

Back in the day, when there were only three networks, everything was targeted to the 18-to-34-year-olds. Today, there is a television station or program for everyone, so it is a lot easier to target your advertising to people who will be interested in your widget. You can get a good idea of the average age of the viewer while watching a television program based on the advertising. For example, if you tune into the nightly news on NBC, CBS or ABC, you will notice that nearly all of the ads are from pharmaceutical companies, targeting Boomers and above. That is because when they grew up, the network 6:30 news was the only place to get your daily input of 'Dirty Laundry.' They still watch today. Same goes for 60-Minutes Sunday nights at 7:00. I have always been fascinated with advertising and I'm even more interested today because of the disruption the internet and mobile devices have created in a relatively short time.

Facebook and Google, for example, are taking targeting to the next level. Marketers can target age, race, sex, interests, issues, zip codes, etc... and have their ad pop up in the "feed." These guys have changed advertising forever, and if you want to reach the Millennials, mobile is where you start.

Millennials do still watch a fair amount of TV, but they are not swayed as easily by advertising like past generations. Research conducted by leading television advertisers found the average person under the age of 30 has a five second attention span when watching television advertisements. This is a major challenge for radio and television advertisers as their model has relied on 60 and 30 second messages for decades. To engage Millennials and most of Gen X, advertising must be entertaining and then be informational. You must grab their attention in the first five seconds or they reach for their remote and time-shift away your message.

If you pay attention to TV advertising like I do, you can see the subtle changes that have transpired. Have you noticed how many commercials feature animals? The animals usually have nothing to do with the product or service, but they are funny, entertaining, and keep you watching.

You can also tell who the advertiser is targeting based on the first five seconds of imaging. Many mainstream ads targeting men will feature beautiful women, even if she is completely disconnected from the product. Ads targeting women will do the same thing, featuring good looking "manly" men doing things they wish their husbands would do. Ads targeting moms, start with cute kid images. Ads targeting Traditionalist don't have to be as quick to the point, but they typically feature "happy times," with family and friends, smiling and enjoying each other's company like the "good old days." I'm not sure why they are always moving in slow motion. I love those pharmaceutical ads that have the happy music and people smiling and moving in slow motion as the voiceover is telling you that one of the side effects is "death!" But every generation loves animals, and they are in a ton of spots today.

Social Media & Reviews

Millennials are heavily influenced by peer reviews from friends and social influencers. By influencers, I don't mean celebrities like actors, athletes and models. Millennials see through them and know they are getting paid tons of cash to promote the products. They will reject them.

By influencers, I mean "experts" in a specific field. Millennial moms, for example, are very influenced by "parenting experts." Millennial moms have been credited for starting the "mommy blogger" revolution where some mom bloggers have hundreds of thousands of social followers. Working with these social influencers in your service or product sector is key.

Millennials expect products and services to have a presence on social media. They will follow brands they like and contribute to the conversations whether they have a good experience or bad. Millennials also expect transparency. If you have someone washing your social media sites by removing all negative posts, it is obvious, and they will reject you. Negative reviews and comments are a gift because they will point out issues you may not know you had. Chances are, if someone takes the time to post a negative comment, there are hundreds of others that feel the same way. Transparency is everything! It is important that you post something daily. If you haven't posted in a while, they will not come back. Embrace all comments, good and especially bad. Thank those who say something nice and immediately respond to negative posts with an apology and a pledge to fix it. Millennials, and anyone following you for that matter, will respect the fact that you accept and address concerns promptly.

Millennials want to have a say in how you run your business, so engage them. Social media gives you the opportunity to throw things out there and ask for feedback. Millennials love to feel like they are contributing to the next color, flavor or new feature.

Millennials Love Coupons

For Boomers and older Gen Xers, the best place to get a good coupon was in the newspaper. Long before the internet gave us access to couponing and discount sites like Groupon, RetailMeNot, and others, the only place you could find a good coupon was in print publications. For decades, the largest circulation day for local newspapers was Thursday.

That was, and still is, the day grocers place their FSIs and coupons.

Being a Gen Xer, my favorite option for coupons, pre-Google, was the Entertainment and Gold C Books. Remember those? What made them awesome was all the killer restaurants that offered two-for-one discounts and the fact that they raised millions of dollars for schools and nonprofit organizations. You could get your money back with one coupon and then have the entire year to save on everything the family did.

My how times have changed. Today, technology has given everyone access to discounts at the touch of their finger and Millennials are leading the charge. Apps like Retail-Me-Not will even notify you of the discount as soon as you walk into a store with a happy cash register sound effect.

Today's Millennials, who were the very elementary school kids selling those Entertainment Books, learned a lot from their parents. Sometimes it was that coupon that made it possible for them to bring a friend along to play miniature golf. Millennials are pragmatic and cost-conscious. They were entering the workforce right around the worst economic downturn since the Great Depression. They saw their parents lose jobs and their retirement savings overnight. They could not find jobs themselves. Times were tough, and every little savings made a difference. Now they find themselves raising their own children, strapped with college loan debt, encouraging them to always look for deals.

Research from PRRI-US Consumer Surveys shows that Millennials are using coupons more than their parents, but they are not getting them from any one source. Instead, they favor online coupons and promo codes over paper coupons. Online coupon usage among Millennials has risen 48% over the past two years. The number of Millennials who reported using mobile coupons to make a purchase rose to 33%, outstripping other generations by a large margin. Another survey by Valassis found that 92% of Millennials use coupons. In the past year, 51% of Millennials said they are using more coupons than the previous year, which is more than Generation X and Baby Boomers.

Millennials also shop with an innate skepticism that they may have inherited from their Gen X parents and older siblings. They don't organically trust brands and, as I mentioned, they can easily see through slick marketing and ad campaigns. Mass distributed coupons alone are not as effective as they were for their parents. Millennials, especially Millennial moms, make purchases based off peer reviews from loyal customers within their trusted centers of influence or social circles.

The Boomers and Gen X'ers lived through times of prosperity and excess. Coupons were not as necessary, and in some cases, you could be seen as "cheap" if you used a coupon. Millennials and the iGens grew up in a time when many people had to find ways to make ends meet, and that included using coupons. Doing so successfully carried with it an image of being smart and savvy.

In summary, make sure you keep these values and customer motivations in mind when marketing to Millennial consumers.

- They desire and value innovation. Never settle. Always improve and improvise.

- They demand instant gratification. They won't wait for you.
- They require customization. Give them the ability to have input on their purchase options.
- They support companies who support diversity and alternative lifestyles. Make sure your advertising and marketing highlights that.
- They are socially responsible and reward companies that openly support charitable causes, community initiatives, and focus on environmental sustainability.
- They use technology, mostly their smartphones to research products, services, company reputations and search for coupons before purchasing, and they will often do it right in front of you.

Millennials at Work

There has been no shortage of press and blogs about the Millennial generation in the workforce. Our company, D. Knight Marketing and Consulting, receives the most interest from organizations wanting help engaging their Millennial employees and customers.

Our Millennial kids have grown up (stop the sarcastic stare). Now they are in the real world and, as an employee, they may need some of the same hand-holding they received as kids. This is very difficult for Boomer and Gen Xer managers to understand and accept, and it is causing tremendous issues in the workplace for leaders and their Millennial employees.

The good news is that the Millennials are the most educated generation ever, according to Pew Research. Many of them completed a full year of college before they graduated from high school. They are extremely capable and will ultimately lead your organization. Despite the negative stereotypes, they do work hard, it just might not be between 9 and 5. They are extremely resourceful and creative. They are extremely loyal, as long as they feel they are growing and making a difference. We will discuss that in detail.

In 2016, Millennials became the largest generation and, by the year 2020, they will represent over 50% of the workforce. 30% of them will be in leadership and management roles. Many of today's businesses and schools are led by Baby Boomers or Gen Xers. A survey of CEOs conducted by Indeed revealed that only 11% have a clear succession plan in place. The numbers don't lie, nearly all the employees climbing into future management roles over the next decade will be Millennials.

In a survey of school superintendents, less than 7% agreed that their school district is doing everything they can to fully understand their Millennial educators and staffers. That is a big issue, considering that nearly all of the new teachers today are Millennials.

As we learned already, many Millennials may not be adequately prepared, lacking the soft skills needed to manage and lead a team or a company. Millennials want to grow and develop their skills. One of the top reasons a Millennial leaves their job is that they feel they are not developing professionally or personally. Millennials won't wait around for things to change. There are no pensions or golden parachutes anymore, so if a Millennial employee isn't happy at the job, they simply leave and find something else. *The 2016 Millennial Impact Report* found that 60% of

Millennials are already planning on leaving their current employer within the next three years. So how do you keep them? It starts with a real understanding of what drives Millennials to excel and succeed.

Despite all of the stereotypes and rhetoric, Millennials aren't that much different than any other employee. They are just less patient with the old way of doing business. Ask any Millennial employee and most will agree on the things that matter to them at work. They want balance, but in a different way than their parent's "work-life-balance." They are looking more for a "work-life-blend." It is important that managers from older generations understand that work can be done effectively from anywhere at any time. To be an effective employee, you no longer need to go into the same office, punch in at 9 and out at 5.

Millennials are the multitasker generation and have amassed great talents, such as using technology to get things done. It is not unusual for a Millennial parent, for example, to leave the office at 3:00 to pick up their kids from school. Take them to soccer, cook dinner, and get them to bed by 8:00. Then they jump back on the laptop or smartphone and effectively work for another four hours at night. You must understand that this generation is always ON. They never turn it off and they are perfectly comfortable sending business communications after hours and even on weekends. Millennials can get it done if you just give them the flexibility and "work-life-blend" they crave.

Millennials know how to use technology to its full potential. They expect their employers to be on the leading edge when it comes to technology. If your company uses dated technology, try to update. In the interim, do not forbid

Millennial employees from using their own devices and technology to get the work done. They also require cutting edge training, meaning they want personal and professional development on everything from systems to soft skills.

I often have Baby Boomer and Gen X clients question investing in new employee (Millennial) training. They don't want to spend the money training them and then "they just leave." I ask them what's worse? Would you rather train them, and they leave, or not train them, and they stay? That usually solicits a long stare, but they get it.

When you develop training for your Millennial employees, don't be selfish. Millennials expect professional development that will help them not only become a better employee, but also a better person. Look beyond training that just benefits the company and provide training that helps them with their soft skills. Conflict resolution, leadership, effective presentation skills, dealing with difficult people, time management, and even stress reduction and meditation practices are well received. If a Millennial employee feels like you are invested in them personally, they will reward you with their loyalty and they will tell everyone how much they love working for you, which helps your future recruiting.

If you treat your Millennial employees badly or provide a negative work experience, your recruiting will suffer immensely. Millennials share everything through their social media platforms, referral websites and apps. They have been doing this since college. Before Millennials, and now the iGens signed up for a particular class in college, they most likely spent a good deal of time on Ratemyprofessors.com, a website that features class and college professor reviews from other students. If a professor is a jerk, everyone knows. If the professor gets glowing reviews, their course will be one of the first to fill the seats.

This same technology is used to rate employers as well. Glassdoor.com features nearly every company in the U.S. Job seekers can find salaries, pros, cons and even reviews of the CEOs. There are even detailed descriptions of real interview experiences, all of which was populated by employees of the company.

Have you looked up your company on Glassdoor.com? You better. It will give you a good look at how your company's employee experience is being communicated to future recruits. If you are giving Millennials a great working experience, they will share (Pro). If you are not, they will share that even more (Con).
Since Millennials have been hard-wired to expect instant gratification, it is no surprise that they will expect to provide instant contribution. They need to know how their work is contributing to the overall success of the organization. They thrive when they possess an ownership mentality. Help them develop that ownership mentality by involving them and connecting their contributions to the bigger picture.

Millennials require clear direction and constant feedback. You can thank their helicopter parents for this one. Annual reviews will fail miserably with this generation. If you give a Millennial a job description and then say, "come back next year and I'll let you know how you are doing," they will leave. I have never liked annual reviews and have always found them ridiculously ineffective. I have been fortunate to have managers that let me know where I stood all the time.

Perhaps it is time for HR departments and managers to seriously rethink the annual review process.

Millennials require regular, even daily, feedback on how they are doing. Your Millennial employees are continually learning. They are already starting off and coming to you as the most educated generation ever. They want opportunities to acquire new skills and grow in their careers. If you do not provide a clear path to where they want to go and give them regular feedback on their progress, they will become frustrated, dissatisfied, and find fulfilling work elsewhere.

I mentioned this earlier and I'll mention it again. One great way to benefit from your new-found age diversity is to start a robust mentoring program that pairs younger workers with more seasoned employees. Don't overlook this benefit. Deloitte Millennial Survey shows that 44% of your youngest employees are considering leaving their current jobs right now and 60% over the next three years. If you don't give Millennials professional development opportunities to help them reach their career and personal goals in a timely fashion, they will find a company who is willing to invest in their future. They will also talk about you on Glassdoor.com.

Millennials as Parents

More than a Million Millennials are becoming moms each year! A whopping 1.3 million Millennials became moms last year, raising the total number of U.S. millennial women who have become mothers to more than 16 million. Most of these moms have children in elementary schools.

As I mentioned, I have more than two decades of experience in working with schools and organizations that include parents and their children as customers and advocates. The next decade will be 'make or break' for these organizations. Parenting styles and communication preferences have changed radically for the Millennial generation. Organizations that attempt to do things "the way they always have" will risk being disrupted into obscurity.

What's different about these Millennial moms versus past generations of parents? The Pew Research Center recently released a survey of Millennial moms. Here is a snapshot of some of the most interesting findings.

- Millennial women are waiting longer to become parents.
- They are shifting away from marriage, with more moms making decisions to raise their kids on their own.
- They have an increased level of educational attainment.
- Many have moved into the labor force, and more are holding management and leadership positions.
- Millennial moms rated "being a good parent" as a top priority, with 52% of Millennial moms saying it was the most important goal in their life above having a successful marriage (only 30%).
- Millennial moms are especially confident in their parenting abilities, with 57% saying they are doing a very good job.

With more and more educated Millennial moms in the workplace and holding key leadership positions, companies and organizations need to offer benefits that do not get in the way of them being the good parent that they strive to be above all else. Since Millennials are waiting longer to become parents, they will be further along in their careers and should have more expendable income. They will also be busier than ever.

Companies with parent-targeted products and services will benefit from these trends if they meet Millennial parents where they are, which includes a strong mobile-only engagement and influencer strategy. Millennial moms will reward companies and new technologies that will save them time by spending more and sharing their positive opinions with their peers through social media.

If your company or organization has products or services that reach Millennial moms, I highly recommend reading the book *"Millennial Moms, 202 Facts Marketers Need to Know to Build Brands and Drive Sales"* by Maria Bailey. Maria has been credited with the practice of "Marketing to Moms." She is an amazing resource and her company, BSM Media, has a variety of effective ways to reach moms, especially Millennial moms. Her book is a must read.

Social Impact is Everything

Think about this for a moment. Millennials were the first generation that was required to perform community service hours in high school to help them graduate and get into a good college. Many had to accumulate as much at 100 hours or more and this amount of service changed them for the better. While they may have hummed and hawed while they were doing it, that "giving back" mindset stuck with them and those values have followed them into adulthood.

Because of that, Millennials won't take any job just for the sake of having a "job." They require passion to be an essential component of their employment. To be passionate, they need to feel like they are making a difference at work. They want to work for companies that stand for more than the bottom line. They value companies that have created grassroots community outreach and well-defined CSR (Corporate Social Responsibility) programs that are woven into the company culture, from the CEO down.

Your CSR must also be home-grown and preferably created with feedback and input from the lowest levels of the organization (and it better include Millennials). I will be the first to agree that there is no mission without margin, but there are many ways to make an impact on your community and the world while also building the bottom line. That is one of the things my company specializes in developing, and "Millennial input" is the secret sauce.

Millennials are very perceptive and can see through company outreach programs that are not sincere and transparent. In the early days of what companies mainly referred to as "community affairs programs," they would simply write a big check to nonprofit organizations, like the Susan G. Komen Foundation, and slap pink ribbons on their packages so that they could allot a shiny page about their great contribution in their annual shareholders report.

While these large foundations and nonprofits do good things, Millennials are more engaged with the "issues," not the "charity." Our company has had great success in helping organizations develop employee-led CSR Action Teams that meet regularly and decide what matters to them, and the company backs them from the top down. Ask your employees what matters to them and let them develop your social impact programs.

Tattoos in the Workplace?

As an expert in intergenerational communication, I constantly remind people that they cannot judge those older or younger based on how it was when they were that age. You can't compare a teen in the 50's with a teen today. Everything is different, and that is why we have the so-called "generation gaps."

Tattoos are one of the most obvious pieces of evidence in regard to these gender gaps. According to Pew Research, over half (54%) of Millennials have done one or more of the following; gotten a tattoo, dyed their hair a nontraditional color, or had a body piercing in a place other than their earlobe. Just over 10% of those over 40 admit to having a tattoo.

Once reserved for indigenous tribes, soldiers, sailors, gang members, and ex-cons, permanent "body art" has become popular and mainstream. Older generations remember seedy tattoo shops being in the ghetto or the "bad part of town." Now, they be found in high-end shopping districts and they look more like an art gallery. It is common to see Millennials, everyone from elite athletes to supermodels, sporting a tattoo (or 12). Tattoos have become so prevalent that the US Navy and other branches of the armed services have changed their policies on the number and size restrictions of tattoos in order to recruit Millennials and iGens.

Companies need to keep this in mind when they are recruiting and interviewing potential Millennial employees. Having a tattoo is as normal and mainstream to Millennials as big hair was to Gen X in the 80s. Letting "body art" affect your decision to hire or not, may cost you the best employee you could ever have.

This trend may not last. We are already seeing evidence of older Millennials showing some "body art" regret. According to a survey conducted by the British Association of Dermatologists, close to a third of the people who get tattoos regret at least one in their collection. Interestingly enough, there's an increased amount of people who are remorseful over tattoos they got when they were 18 to 25 years old. 45% of the survey's respondents said the ink they wanted to get rid of most was art they acquired in the period of their life most characterized by youth and impulsivity. As a result, and somewhat ironically, the tattoo-removal business is one the fastest growing industries in the developed world today. So, while it's painful and expensive, as it turns out, today's permanent decisions aren't so permanent after all.

Tips to Managing Millennials

In summary, Millennial employees are educated, tech savvy, and socially responsible, but they require regular guidance, feedback, and encouragement.

Here are ten tips to help you successfully engage, motivate, and manage your Millennial team members.

1. As a manager, possess a "replace yourself" mentality - coach your Millennial employees to eventually lead the organization.
2. During the hiring process, be very clear with expectations, duties, work environment, hours, dress code, etc.

3. Have an immediate onboarding plan for the current job.
4. Have a personal and professional development plan in place for future opportunities.
5. Show them opportunities to grow and be very clear on what it takes to get there.
6. Be extremely clear with expectations and results.
7. Provide constant feedback, encouragement, and hold them accountable.
8. Enlist their support in helping solve company challenges.
9. Be very open to flexible schedules and virtual work environments - make sure you have accountability and identifiable measurements in place.
10. Sponsor employee (non-work) interest clubs to encourage camaraderie outside the office.
11. Organize community charity events and ask your Millennial employees for input from the start.
12. Get out of your office - walk the floor, check in every day, and see how things are going. Give out daily encouragement "atta-boys" (or girls).
13. Provide constructive feedback, including public recognition for a job well done - and do it often.
14. Be very transparent – tell the truth and don't hide anything. They will know.
15. Constantly explain the WHY – help them understand why decisions were made.

Chapter 7

Generation Z - The iGen
Born After 1995

"Wish we could turn back time, to the good
old days. When our momma sang us to
sleep, but now we're stressed out. Wish we
could turn back time, to the good old days.
When our momma sang us to sleep, but
now we're stressed out.
We're stressed out."
"Stressed Out" – Twenty-One Pilots

Sign Posts That Shaped Generation Z – iGen

- Digital natives – don't remember a time without the internet and mobile phones
- Introduction of the iPhone
- Growth in social media: Facebook, then Instagram and Snapchat
- 9/11 Attacks
- 2008 Great Recession and aftermath
- Terrorism – don't not remember a time without war
- Hurricane Katrina
- Mental illness epidemic - anxiety and depression
- Opioid epidemic
- Obama Presidential term
- 2016 Presidential election
- Donald Trump as a celebrity & President
- Fake news

If you are running a business and have picked up this book to help you learn the best management strategies for your age diverse workforce, you may be thinking you can skip this chapter. Maybe Generation Z hasn't even entered your radar unless you employee teens or have products and services that target teens or schools.

I encourage you to read on. I believe Gen Z will be a disruptive force in the workplace and across the world. I am more excited about the potential for Gen Z than any previous generation.

Parents should also read on. If you are raising teens or will be raising them soon, you will learn some interesting things in this chapter. I can proudly say that fully understanding our youngest generation the way I do, has helped me become a better parent to my Gen Z/Millennial Cusper son. By the time you finish this chapter, you will likely be awestruck by the amount of change and distress our teens and children have experienced in their short time on earth. As parents and employers, we must be prepared for our future workforce. They will be more diverse than ever and will feel they have to solve some of the worst environmental, social, and economic problems in history.

In 2006, there were a record number of births in the U.S. Forty-nine percent of those born were Hispanic. This is rapidly changing the American melting pot in terms of behavior and culture. Since the early 1700's, the most common last name in the U.S. was "Smith," now it is "Rodriguez." The number of births in 2006 far outnumbered the beginning of the Baby Boomer Generation, so it is clear that Gen Z will become the largest generation, surpassing the Millennials in population by the mid-2020s. If you think the Millennials were different, Gen Z is going to be a whole new and exciting challenge and opportunity.

For this chapter, I'll be referring to data and research conducted by generational author and psychologist, Jean Twenge. Twenge uses survey data from 11 million young people that has been consistently collected since the 1960s and 1970s. She also uses hundreds of focus groups and has conducted deep-dive interviews with Millennial and Gen Z teens. It is important to not judge other generations using your own generational preferences alone. It is best to study different generations based on the historical context of their formative years. By utilizing historical survey data, Twenge identifies some clear generational changes and differences. I certainly won't plagiarize her work, but I will tell you that there are not many people, in my opinion, that understand our youngest generations better that Dr. Jean Twenge.

Jean Twenge recently released her new book about Generation Z, *"iGen, Why Today's Super-Connected Kids Are Growing Up Less Rebellious, More Tolerant, Less Happy--and Completely Unprepared for Adulthood—And What That Means for the Rest of Us."* If you are interested in how today's teens will become productive members of the workforce, if you work with teens in schools, or if you are a parent of a teen, I highly encourage you to add Twenge's book to your reading wish list.

I first started following Twenge's writing back in 2006. That is when she authored a book about Millennials before everyone else jumped on the bandwagon. I am referring to her book titled, *"Generation Me: Why Today's Young Americans Are More Confident, Assertive, Entitled--and More Miserable Than Ever Before."*

There are still robust discussions about what to name our youngest generation. Many, including *Forbes* are asking their readers and contributors to chime in on what the generation following the Millennials should be named. Forbes even ran a contest, asking for suggestions and the winning name was *"The Homeland Generation,"* primarily because of all the historical events around homeland security that have occurred in the past fifteen years. This generation has grown up seeing the attacks of 9/11, the War on Terror, attacks on the homeland, etc. I am thinking that our digitally native teens won't be excited about being named after a big government agency, the TSA, in those cool blue shirts at the airport, patting down grandma in her wheelchair.

Of course, Generation Z has been used the most, primarily because it comes after Generation Y. Again, very creative. If Millennials shunned the use of "Y" because they didn't want to be connected to Gen Xers, then Y is dead, and they will forever be known as those dang Millennials. If more people accept the term "Millennial," then "Gen Z" makes no sense. I think the Homeland Generation is ridiculous.

The best name I have heard was created by Twenge and that is "iGen." This makes the most sense to me and many others because of the massive influence smartphones, and social media have had on our youngest cohorts. The use of "i" also makes sense because the iPhone was introduced in 2007 in iGen's prime formative years. Today, three out of every four teens own an iPhone. With that said, I'm with Jean and will be calling these youngsters iGen going forward.

Are iGens Just Baby Millennials?

It is easy to lump iGen in with the Millennials, but that would be a mistake. Prior to 2012, the Cuspers and those born a few years after their generational change year were very similar to their predecessors. To a degree, the oldest iGens, born from around 1995 to 2003, did have a lot of similarities to the Millennials at first. That changed in 2012, when Twenge's iGen research started to see some trending "spikes" instead of the traditional bell curves like she had been observing for the past decades. So what happened in 2012?

2012 was the year that smartphones hit critical mass with teens, meaning that more than 50% of teens owned a smartphone. It was around 2012 that we started to notice seismic shifts in teen behaviors and their emotional

93

wellbeing. Once most teens owned smartphones, their use of social media apps like Facebook, Instagram and Snapchat took off as well. Everything changed in 2012 and it became obvious that this would be the generation most shaped by smartphones and social media. You might say teens turned it on in 2012 and haven't been able to turn it off since.

Now that some iGens are starting to make their way through college and into the workforce, we are noticing some clear differences from the Millennials. Millennials may have felt they were being forced to grow up too fast and in some cases, like their Gen X and Boomer parents, maybe they did.

The common thought is that technology and the ongoing access to the world wide web is shrinking our world and causing kids to grow up faster than previous generations. Many feel kids don't get to be kids anymore because of their constant exposure to adult news and issues. For iGens, this could not be farther from the truth. In reality, they are growing up slower than past generations, by choice. They are postponing the common rights of adolescence, avoiding "adulting" at all cost.

Invented by Millennials and iGens, "adulting" is a verb used to describe a boring, tedious task, typically associated with being an adult. #adulting usually trends on social media on Sunday nights, as Millennials publicly share their frustration with having to go back to work on Monday. *"Awesome time at the #Earthday festival today, back to my exciting #adulting cube tomorrow."* Is that a stereotype? Isn't Earth Day the Millennial's favorite day of the year? Stop it! Just kidding.

Twenty-somethings will also use the hashtag #adulting to make fun of anything they must do that resembles adult responsibility. They can be quite humorous. Hey, I get it. I just crossed 50 and I can relate to a lot of the posts.

Here is one of my favorites from @yaddathree: "99% of being an adult is looking for an adultier adult to do the adulting." #adulting

All joking aside, iGen is growing up slower and postponing adulting. There are a few real examples from Jean Twenge's iGen research on some radical differences in how iGens spend their time, versus the way Millennial and Gen Xers spent their leisure time as teens.

The allure of independence, which was essential for past generations, is not nearly as important to today's teens. For those of us that grew up in the 70s and 80s, this seems bizarre. We could not wait to gain our independence. Like me, I am sure many of you were at the DMV the day you turned 16. The driver's license was the ultimate form of independence. No longer did we have to rely on mom or dad to cart us around. We could go wherever we wanted to go as long as we were home by the designated "curfew." To older generations like mine, a driver's license equaled freedom.

As I stated many times before, the goal of intergenerational engagement is not to fall back on the nostalgia of "the way things used to be," it is to understand how they are now. Driving, the symbol of Gen X independence and freedom, is not that big of a deal for iGens. Nearly all of Boomer high school students had their driver's license by the spring of their senior year. Today, more than one in four teens still lack having a driver's license at the time of their high school graduation. "Mom… Can you drive me to my graduation party?" Huh?

When Twenge interviewed teens that got their driver's licenses after high school graduation, the teens described getting their license as something that they were nagged into by their parents. There comes a time in every mom and dad's life when we put an abrupt end to being our kid's 24-7 Uber driver. For Gen Xers, it was the other way around. We nagged our parents to take us to the DMV when it opened on the day of our sweet 16. We drove our parents home and dropped them off.

Another stark difference found by Twenge is that today's teens are less likely to date. Only about 56 percent of high school seniors in 2015 went on dates. For Boomers and Gen Xers, the number was over 85 percent. The decline in dating, coincides with the postponement of sexual activity for iGens as well. The sharpest drop is with 9th graders, among whom the number of sexually active teens has dropped by almost 40 percent since 1991. There are some good trends that come from this. The teen birth rate hit an all-time low in 2016, down a whopping 67 percent since its peak in 1991.

Less teens and iGens are working part time jobs. In an information-based economy that places a value on higher education above early work history, more parents are inclined to encourage their kids to stay home and "study hard" instead of finding a part-time job. When Gen X grew up, we went out whenever we could. We had to work so that we could afford all of the things we needed to support our new-found independence. We needed money for gas, food, dates, beer, etc... and our parents were not paying for it without completing a laundry list of chores. Teens don't leave the house as much today, so they don't need the extra spending money. It seems that today's teens are cool with being "home bodies" primarily because their social life is lived on their smartphone. They no longer need to leave home to spend time with their friends.

Teens today are more comfortable in their bedrooms than in a car or at a party. Because of this, today's teens are physically safer than teens have ever been. Less teen drivers equates to less car accidents. Less teens at parties equates to less incidences of alcohol consumption. Today's teens are less likely to leave the house without their parents. Twelfth graders in 2015 were going out less often than eighth-graders did as recently as 2009.

While iGen may be physically safer, psychologically, today's teens are more vulnerable than the Millennials were as teens. According to The Centers for Disease Control and Prevention, the rates of teen depression and suicide have escalated dramatically since 2011. It is not a stretch to say that iGens are on the brink of the worst mental health crisis in decades. You can thank smartphones and social media for this silent epidemic.

Generation Stress: Mental Illness, a Silent Epidemic

In our intergenerational engagement consulting, most of our work focuses on helping Gen X and Baby Boomer corporate leaders learn how to recruit, engage, inspire, and retain Millennial employees. In my conversations with human resource directors, the topic of their Millennial employee's challenges with anxiety, depression, and mental health almost always comes up. It is true that many Millennials are struggling with work related anxiety and depression, primarily caused by disconnected work environments that are not addressing their most basic personal needs and aspirations. Other causes can be attributed to the way they were brought up, as discussed in the previous chapter. Some may argue that Millennials lack the soft skills required to thrive in traditional workplace settings.

Thanks to smartphones and social media, mental health challenges have been dramatically magnified with iGens. Many, including myself, believe that mental illness is a silent epidemic, especially for teens and young adults. While there has been some progress in the areas of awareness and treatment, there is still a lot of negative social stigma around the topic of mental illness. Even with the National Institute of Mental Health finding that 50 percent of all students age 14 and older with a mental illness drop out of school, risk-averse school districts are slow to respond, often not offering ample support networks until after one of their students commits suicide.

The NIMH statistics are telling. One in five youth suffer from a diagnosed mental health condition like anxiety, depression, or bipolar disorder. As many as 80 percent of adolescents indicate that they have experienced some form of mild to moderate anxiety or depression. While there are a host of internal and external causes of mental illness, many have blamed smartphones and social media for elevating the problem. Fifty percent of all lifetime cases of mental illness begin by age 14, about four years after the average iGen receives their first smartphone and two years after they can "legally" obtain social media accounts from Facebook, Instagram, Snapchat and others.

There is compelling evidence that screen time is a major contributing factor to elevated mental health issues. The National Institute of Drug Abuse funds the "Monitoring the Future" survey. The survey has asked 12th graders over 1,000 questions per year since 1991. Some of the questions are designed to assess how happy teens are. The survey also asks how much of their leisure time they spend on various activities. Some of the activities they ask about are non-screen activities such as in-person social interaction and exercise. In recent years, they have also been asking about screen-based activities like using social media, texting, playing video games, and searching the internet. The results are clear and telling. Teens that spend an above average amount of time with screen-based activities are more likely to be unhappy. Teens that spend more time than average on non-screen activities are happier.

Tom Kersting is a renowned psychotherapist, long-time high school counselor, and author of the book "Disconnected." Kersting's new book explores the device-dependent world our children live in and how it is impacting their mental and emotional well-being. He discusses research that shows that spending too much time in the cyber world is rewriting kids' brains and affecting their ability to flourish in the real world as anxiety, depression, and attention issues soar. In a recent conversation with Kersting, he told me he has counseled more middle-school aged children for major anxiety disorders in the past year than he has over the past sixteen years combined. Kersting and many others are convinced screen-time is to blame.

The average teen is spending nine hours per day in front of a screen. This is more than any other activity, including sleep. Kersting says, "This is a perfect storm. The human brain cannot handle nine hours of any activity, much less activities that thrust you into a virtual world that is constantly telling you that you are not good enough. Nine hours a day, 63 hours per week, 3,276 hours per year. The equivalent of 136 days, or a third of the year, disengaged from reality and comparing themselves to others. Kersting says, "All this is happening when children's minds are developing. It will have lasting impacts on their futures."

In "Disconnected," Kersting discusses how screen time physiologically changes your brain, and how the social media companies know that. They are not your friend. Kersting asks, "Because kids of this generation spend so much time using powerful electronic devices, their brains were changing, something known as neuroplasticity. Neuroplasticity is the brain's ability to reorganize itself by forming new neural connections, leaving behind past traits and developing new ones. Could all of this "screen time" be changing kids' brains, thereby causing older children to display inattentiveness, lack of focus, and disorganization - all symptoms of ADHD?"

In Kersting's home state of New Jersey, where he is a high school counselor, he tells me about the state's focus on the one-to-one model. One-to-one is when every student in a school, or school district, has a laptop or portable screen. This is a monumental push throughout public education. School districts are very "me too" driven. They often look at what other districts are doing and strive to do the same. This is discussed in greater detail in the Education chapter.

While I am not going to debate the effectiveness of every child having a laptop, Kersting maintains that this is a disaster. "Research proves again and again that children, and adults for that matter, learn better with pen, paper, and a focus on the teaching. When every child is head down in a laptop in the classroom, it is impossible for them to focus on the teacher." When I spoke at the National Principals Conference in 2017, I noticed that a lot of the subject matter was on technology and ed-tech. In the exhibition hall, there were over 300 companies trying to get educators to buy their products and services. Over two-thirds of those companies were tech-based.

I believe ed-tech can provide some wonderful new solutions to the everyday problems that educators are facing. In full disclosure, many of our clients are Israeli and Silicon Valley-based ed-tech companies. I also believe in the power of reading a book, taking notes with a pen and paper, and intently listening to a compelling lecturer. There are very expensive private schools that feel the same way.

New York University professor, Adam Alter, author of "Irresistible: The Rise of Addictive Technology and the Business of Keeping Us Hooked," discusses The Waldorf School in Silicon Valley. The Waldorf School has 160 locations and they proudly shun the use of technology.

Alter says in his book, "There's a school in Silicon Valley that doesn't allow the use of any tech. It's called the Waldorf School and it's fascinating because the school has no computers, no iPads, and no iPhones. They try to minimize tech altogether; therefore, people enjoy a lot of time face-to-face and they also go outside a lot. What's interesting about this school is that 75% of the students there are the children of Silicon Valley tech execs. This is striking. These are people who, publicly, will expound on the wonders of the products they're producing, and, at the same time, they

101

decided in all their wisdom that their kids didn't belong in a school that used that same tech." Apparently, many Silicon Valley execs also believe technology may not be the end-all solution to their own children's education, but they are more than willing to push it on yours. Parents beware.

Since 2012, the "Monitoring the Future Survey" found that all screen activities are linked to less happiness, and all non-screen activities are linked to more happiness. There is not a single exception. The survey found that eighth-graders who spend 10 or more hours per week on social media are 56 percent more likely to say they are unhappy than those who spend less of their leisure time interacting on social media. Even those who spend just six hours per week are 47 percent more likely to be miserable. The survey also found the exact opposite to be true for those teens who spend an above average amount of time hanging out with their friends in person. They are 20 percent less likely to say they are unhappy than those who hang out with friends less.

iGens that spend the most time on social media sites are the most likely to admit that they feel lonely as well. They often feel left out of things and say they "wish they had more good friends." Teen's feelings of loneliness peaked in 2013, after the 2012 smartphone boom and have remained high since.

Feeling unhappy and lonely is a recipe for depression. Social media enabled "FOMO" or "fear of missing out" can trigger severe social and anticipatory anxiety. Today's teens may go to fewer parties and spend less time socializing in person. When they do party in person or hangout together they document every second on Snapchat, Instagram, and Facebook. If you weren't invited to the party, you know it instantly, and that can trigger intense FOMO, anxiety, and depression. FOMO is more serious and damaging for girls. In the survey, 48 percent more girls said they often felt left out in 2015 than in 2010, compared with 27 percent more boys. This makes sense because girls use social media more often, giving them more opportunities to experience FOMO when they see their classmates and friends doing things together without them.

The anxiety and depression triggered by social media not only occurs when teens are reading other's posts, it happens when they post themselves as well. Many iGens feel their popularity is elevated or diminished based on the number of "likes" or comments they receive on their social media posts. When Gen Xers were teens, popularity was mostly based on looks, social status, and whether you were voted onto the homecoming court or elected class president. It took a lot of work back then to gain that popularity status and it's no different today. Teens will put an enormous amount of effort into building their social status, making sure they are "posting" their right foot forward.

Today, those with the most social media "friends" and those who get the most "likes" are the most popular. I have seen teens in the schools I work in post something on social media and check it every ten seconds to monitor the number of likes, comments, and shares. The quest is to be part of the "100 Club." Yes, that is a thing. You gain admittance into the 100 club if all of your social media posts reach a minimum of 100 likes. iGens will regularly delete a post that doesn't reach 100 likes in a short amount of time because it makes them look less popular. Social media posts that don't get a lot of "likes" can make teens feel rejected. Over time, repeated feelings of social media rejection can lead to depression and anxiety.

I live close to the beach near a popular spring break destination in Florida. I am always amused by watching groups of teens, usually girls, standing in the waves posing for the perfect "selfie." It almost looks like a mini-photoshoot. They will take a selfie and gather around the phone to look at the result. "Not good enough!" They group together again, and again until they all agree "that's the one." Then one of the girls posts the perfectly executed selfie on Instagram and "tags" her friends. After all, they were there and not "left out."

iGens extreme focus on posting the perfect photos creates a fake reality. I like to call it "fakebook." The "fakebook" lives that teens go out of their way to broadcast to the world are a major contributor to iGen's mental health crisis. The average iGen is forced to compare everyone else's highlight reels to their reality. It can be a constant reminder that everyone you know is prettier, happier, having more fun, and is more popular than you. It's simply not true, but perception is reality for many iGens and that can be very depressing and damaging.

Another iGen trend is that they are getting less sleep during a time of their lives that they need it most. The National Sleep Foundation says teens should get about nine hours of sleep per night. A teen who is getting less than seven hours of sleep per night is significantly sleep deprived. The Monitoring the Future survey found that 57 percent more teens were sleep deprived in 2015 than in 1991. Jean Twenge interviewed hundreds of iGen teens and discussed what they did with their smartphones when they went to bed. Those of us who are raising teens today, will not be surprised by her findings.

Nearly all of the teens Twenge interviewed admitted that they sleep with their phones, putting them under their pillow, on the mattress, or at the very least, within arm's reach of the bed. To their credit, most of them used their phones as alarm clocks, but checking social media was the primary task. They checked social media before they went to sleep, and it was the first thing they reached for when they woke the next day. Their phone is the last thing they see before they fall asleep and the first thing they see when they wake up. If they wake during the middle of the night, they often check it then as well.

There is evidence that screen time negatively affects quality of sleep. Of all screens, the smartphone is the worst culprit because they project "blue light" which emulates daylight and reduces the body's ability to produce melatonin, nature's sleep aid. If most teens are sleeping with their phones and taking in high doses of blue light right before bed, this must be affecting their sleep. Note, this is a serious issue for iGens and Millennials, but it is also affecting older generations as well. I know a beautiful Gen Xer, who will remain nameless, that sleeps with her iPhone one foot from our, urrr, her head at night.

Sleep deprivation is linked to a host of issues, including compromised thinking and reasoning, increased illness, weight gain, and high blood pressure. Those who don't get enough sleep are much more prone to depression, anxiety, and other mental health issues. Could smartphones be causing teens to lose sleep, which then leads to depression? Or maybe it is the other way around, with the smartphones causing the depression which leads to sleep deprivation. Regardless, the smartphone with its blue light and audible alerts is likely playing a role in both.

The effects of increased screen time on iGens cannot be ignored. The more time teens spend on their smartphones, the more likely they are to report symptoms of depression and anxiety. Eighth graders who are heavy users of social media increase their risk of depression by 27 percent. Teens that focus their leisure time on non-screen after school activities like playing sports, participating in service clubs, reading books, or even doing homework more than the average teen, cut their depression risks significantly.

A sobering consequence of higher depression and anxiety in teens is a higher incidence of teen suicide. The percentage of teens attempting suicide over the last decade has increased significantly for both sexes; however, teen girl's recent suicide rates have been climbing faster than boys. Three times as many 12-to-14-year-old girls committed suicide in 2015 as in 2007. The suicide success rate for boys remains higher primarily because they tend to use more lethal methods, but the girls are catching up fast. The dramatic rise in iGen girl suicides could be attributed to cyberbullying, as we discussed earlier, which tends to affect girls more than boys.

Here's a stunning statistic that indirectly captures the connection between iGen's social isolation and suicide: Since 2007, the homicide rate among teens has dropped, but the suicide rate has climbed. As teens have started to spend more time alone in their rooms and less time together, they have become less likely to kill one another, but more likely to kill themselves. In 2012, for the first time in 24 years, the teen suicide rate was higher than the teen homicide rate.

iGens as Consumers

Generation X was the first to leverage the internet to shop for products and services. They forced companies to develop online marketing and sales strategies. They also were the first to demand a lot of options and customization. Millennials changed the playbook when it came to consumerism, primarily because they were the first generation that understood how to leverage social media to research, shop, and review everything before they made a purchase. They were also not afraid to post negative reviews when they were not happy with their purchase. Millennials created the "consumer driven" economy. It took a while for retailers and other companies to figure out how to engage Millennials. They were different in the way they responded to advertising and marketing and eventually wanted most of their purchase options to be accessed through the web and, ultimately, through their smartphones. Millennials helped Amazon go from a book seller to a seller of "everything."

As you have learned in this chapter already, iGens are not baby Millennials, and that goes for the way they will shop as well. Over the next decade, iGens will cause legacy products and categories to be disrupted again and again - similar to the way the Millennials created the "sharing economy" that elevated Uber and Airbnb to billion-dollar companies. Do you think that 10 years ago, Hilton or Marriott ever envisioned a competitor that would steal massive market share without owning a single hotel room?

Many companies have been disrupted by the "KGOY" phenomenon, aka, "Kids Growing Older Younger." While iGen is postponing adulthood and adult responsibilities, they are disrupting childhood mainstays like the toy industry. The use of computers, tablets, smartphones and web-based learning has grown exponentially. Because of that, iGen children leave behind toys at a much younger age than previous generations.

A good example is what is happening at Mattel, the maker of Barbie dolls. In the early 1900's the average age of a child in their target market was 10 years old. In 2000 it dropped to three years old. As children reach the age of four or five, and are old enough to play on the computer, tablet, or their parent's smartphone, they become less interested in toys and begin to desire electronics such as cell phones and video games.

Reading printed books "for pleasure" is quickly becoming another iGen casualty. While there has been some growth in eBooks with iGens that can be accessed on smartphones, tablets, or e-readers, less of them are reading for pleasure. In Twenge's research, she found that less than 16 percent of teens have read a book for pleasure in the past year. In the mid 1970's over 80 percent of teens indicated that they had read at least one book for pleasure over the past year. Reading has also suffered because of the decline in attention spans for Millennials and now iGens. Millennials decreased their average attention spans down to 12 seconds and now iGens are down to an 8 second attention span - 1 second less than a goldfish. Smartphones with high speed, instant access to everything in the world is much more interesting than grinding through all 281 pages of Harper Lee's, *"To Kill a Mockingbird."*

After working in and around schools in the children's publishing industry for more than two decades, this disturbs me. There is no shortage of research that shows how independent reading develops lifelong skills. Unfortunately, I don't feel that schools are promoting independent reading and its incredible benefits. I see too many schools that still assign the class a novel that everyone in the same grade must read. This takes away choice. While a few students may enjoy the experience of reading the assigned novel, most will see it as "work" and may associate the act of reading as something that they "have" to do, not "want" to do. That is likely to follow them into adulthood.

There are some exceptions, especially in elementary schools. Several school districts, including Marion County in Florida, have banned traditional homework in favor of assigning 20 minutes of independent reading per night instead. Reading for fun is their homework. This only works if the child is allowed the opportunity to select their own books. Hopefully, this is a trend that will grow. Something as simple as teaching a young, digitally native iGen to focus on reading for twenty minutes per day in their formative years can be life-changing. If we can introduce young iGens to the joys of independent reading in their formative years, I can't help but think that they will enter adolescence more mentally prepared to tackle the world of smartphones and social media.

It is obvious that Millennials, and now the iGens, are already disrupting some of the long-standing bellwether brands, products, and services that their Gen X and Boomer parents helped create. There are some that are obvious and there will be others that we haven't thought of yet, but it is inevitable. There is not one industry that is safe from generational disruption. If you think you are safe, you are dead.

The sign posts that shaped iGens have certainly altered their consumer patterns and preferences. Their most influential sign post was the Great Recession of 2008 and the residual effects that lasted years after. iGens witnessed their parents being laid off and having their pensions and 401(k) plans wiped out. Maybe they lost their home or had friends that lost their homes. Even though they were young at the time, the family and economic tension left scars that drastically altered the way they feel about money. Those scars impact not only how they spend their own money, but also how they influence their parent's purchasing decisions for the family.

J. Walter Thomas Intelligence conducted consumer research with iGens in 2014. Since younger iGens do not have a lot of expendable income, they specifically looked at how they influence family purchases. For example, they found that 90 percent of iGens will make sure their parents feel a planned purchase is affordable before going ahead with it. Sixty-four percent said their parents paid for the purchase with their credit/debit card.

When it comes to spending their own money, more than 50 percent identify themselves as deal hunters. This explains the recent rebirth of couponing as an effective marketing strategy. Fifty-seven percent of iGens research products on their smartphones before making a purchase. Their favorite things to spend money on, in order of preference are: food and drink, going out with friends, and clothes. Unlike Millennials who became online shopping experts and helped Amazon rise to its dominance, iGens are headed back to the mall. They like to visit brick-and-mortar retailers. Since iGens are very frugal with their money, they want to do everything they can to make sure what they are buying is good quality and will last. They will read peer reviews online, but when it comes to the eventual purchase, they are more likely to go to the store so they can see, touch, and feel for themselves before purchasing.

Believe it or not, iGens are even thinking about retirement and investing, most likely because they experienced their parent's financial meltdown in the Great Recession. They don't want the same fate. In the JWT research, 57 percent of iGens would rather save money than spend it. Seventy-six percent spend money on themselves, while 62 percent save it. Thirty-eight percent spend money on things for friends and family and 10 percent plan to give their money to charity. Their top financial goals are buying a car, paying for education, and buying a house.

In many ways, iGen's values and characteristics are more in line with their Baby Boomer grandparents, rather than the Millennials.

Here are a few examples of the way iGens differ from the typical Millennial consumer and ways you can use those differences to reach iGens.

Millennials	iGen	Reaching iGen
-Idealistic -Optimistic -Grew up in an economic boom	-More Pragmatic -Grew up in a recession	-Focus on long term value -Provide opportunities to see, feel your products
-Spend money on experiences -Enjoy the entire experience of buying	-Saving money -Want their purchases to maximize every dollar -They know money can run out	-Demonstrate how your products are a good value for their spending -Utilize discounts and coupons
-Wants brands to be transparent	-Taking brand transparency to the next level -Rejects over polished content	-Utilize, non-celebrity influencer marketing -Be transparent and honest on social media
-Shops online like a pro -Abandoned the mall	-Likes to shop in retail locations -Wants to see, touch and feel to make sure their purchase is high quality	-Offer in-store educational or entertainment experiences
-Wanted to be defined by brands -Collaborators	-They are their own brand -Celebrate independence	-Celebrate the individual -Don't prescribe a specific image

iGens as Employees

Our newest generation is starting to enter the workforce, and it's one that employers will need to prepare for. Unless you are in the retail or restaurant business with part-time teen employees today, you might not be thinking about recruiting iGens. Keep in mind that the iGens are 23 million strong and will flood the job market by the end of the decade. It is predicted that they will also surpass their Millennial predecessors in size by the mid 2020's.

Now that you know iGen's are the first digital natives, you must realize that your mobile presence is everything for iGens and most Millennials, for that matter. As a corporate recruiter in today's market, you can no longer focus on the empty positions you need to fill today. You must also work on the empty positions you will have to fill ten years from today.

Today's high school teens are already engaged in the economy. They are taking college courses. They are volunteering and even doing summer internships. Many high schools force students to choose career paths and majors by the time they reach the 10th grade. Boomers and Gen Xers were different. Some of us may have known what we wanted to do after high school, but most of us who went to college, started without a clue. We just left home, started college, and our parents said, "You'll figure out what you want to do someday." Even when we thought we had a plan and declared a major, we often changed it midstream and had to prescribe to the "five-year plan" (which my dad was thrilled about). That was the Gen Xer's way of avoiding "adulting."

Because of the intense pressure on today's teens to proclaim what they want to do for the rest of their lives, before they can even legally drive, they are looking at your company right now. Many high school guidance programs require students, as early as the 9th grade, to do research and reports on companies they may be interested in working for one day. How do they do that? You guessed it, they are visiting your website, and they are doing it on their smartphones. You have a unique ability to use your website to publicize great things about your company that are important to not only today's recruits, but tomorrow's as well. Teens will remember what they read about you when it's time to start sending out resumes.

iGens will also remember how their experience was on your website, so it better be mobile optimized. In 2017, I shouldn't have to be saying this, but it is frightening to me that so many large companies still don't get this. A good percentage of Millennial and iGen's interactions with your web presence is going to be through their smartphones. That's everyone under the age of 40. They are very tech savvy. It is not a stretch to assume that as much as 75 percent of your online interaction is coming from iGens and Millennials, unless you sell those slow-motion pharmaceuticals. If a Millennial or iGen has to pinch and zoom their smartphone screens to be able to read and navigate your page, they will not stay. They will also tell themselves that your company is in the stone age, and that will affect their decision to work for you in the future.

With that said, you should make sure you have a dedicated section for your social impact and corporate social responsibility (CSR). Don't make them look for it. As you have learned, social impact is extremely important for

114

younger generations, so give back and promote it in an authentic way. iGens and Millennials want to know what it is like to work for you. There should be a section on your site that talks about your company culture, vision and mission. This section should feature testimonials from current employees, touting what they love about working for your company.

As mentioned before, pay attention to employee recruiting and employer review sites like Glassdoor, Kununu, and others. If your disgruntled employees post negative reviews, it will ultimately affect whether prospects pursue employment with you. As a rule, these reviews tend to identify cultural issues that you must take seriously. Encourage your happy employees, current or past, to post positive reviews about their experience working for your company. Yes, there may be the occasional bad employee that you just can't please.

To attract young employees, your company must have a strong presence on every social networking platform. If you can't do all of them, start with Facebook, Instagram and Pinterest. You must also be "active." You can't simply create a Facebook page and not post and promote daily. Social media savvy iGens and most Millennials will look at the date of your last post and if it's more than a week old, they won't come back.

It is critical that you hire a full-time employee to manage your social media. Don't be that company that reaches out to one of their "young and hip" new employees and says, "In addition to your day-to-day responsibilities that we hired you for, we would like you to handle our social media." Bad idea. If you do not have the luxury to hire a full time social media person, there are many companies that you can contract with that can run your social media effectively.

To attract iGens and Millennials, your social media and marketing must be as transparent as possible. I have mentioned this before and I'm repeating it because it's important. If you get negative feedback on your website or social media sites, don't censor it. Address it publicly and leave the interaction in your "feed." Younger consumers and potential employees appreciate the fact that you admit that you are not perfect and that you address customer complaints head on. If your entire social media feed looks like a love fest with nothing but glowing reviews and comments, they will see through that and develop a skeptical perception of your organization and products.

In 2016, Monster Worldwide, a global leader in connecting people to jobs, conducted their inaugural Monster Multi-Generational Survey. The study surveyed more than 2,000 people across the Boomer, Gen X, Y, and Z generations. The Gen Z (iGen) respondents pre-qualified themselves as either employed or, planning to work in the future. While iGens haven't been in the professional workplace long, here is what we know so far about how they would like to be managed and what you can do now to recruit iGens.

The study found that digitally native iGens don't just think outside the box, they ignore the box entirely. As they strive to reinvent the norms, iGens will be attracted to careers that have both purpose and pragmatism. Seventy-four percent of iGens believe jobs should have a greater meaning than just getting a paycheck. "Passion before paycheck!" Millennials started this trend and iGen is advancing it further. Millennials were the first generation required to perform

116

community service to graduate. iGens are still required to do so, but they are doing 2-to-3 times more community service to help them stand out in the college application process.

It is true that iGens want passion in their careers, but paychecks are equally important. iGens are driven by money and ambition. While the Monster survey found that iGen was motivated by a variety of factors, one thing stood out. They will do whatever it takes to reach their goals.

Entrepreneurship is a big deal for iGens. A global study by Monster found that seventy-six percent of them see themselves as owners of their own careers and driving their own professional advancement. Nearly half of them want to have their own business, compared to just 32 percent across the rest of the working generations. It is important that you feed their entrepreneurial spirit with intrapreneurship opportunities within your business. Challenge them and assign them to new business opportunities.

Sixty-seven percent are willing to relocate for a good job. They carry their friends with them in their pockets, so leaving town is no big deal. Since iGens are connected to their smartphones to the point that they even sleep with them, they are not opposed to working outside the traditional 9-to-5 workday hours. Fifty-eight percent are open to working nights and weekends for a better salary, compared to 41 percent of their Gen X parents.

Are we experiencing a flashback or #ThrowbackThursday? You probably are noticing that many of the iGen values and characteristics seem to align better with Traditionalists and Boomers, rather than the Millennials. While Millennials valued ping-pong, nap pods, and free lunch, iGens value the benefits and security that have traditionally been associated with Boomers and Gen Xers. The Monster study revealed that iGen's top three "must haves" were health insurance (70%), a competitive salary (63%), and a boss they respect (61%).

It is no surprise that technology is very important to iGens and this will carry into the workplace. Fifty-seven percent of iGens feel that technology allows them to be more productive and mobile. Furthermore, 39 percent see their smartphones as essential, compared to 25 percent across all working generations. As you learned from iGens as teens, the smartphone allows them to be "always on." This will continue into their career. They will determine their own schedules and create tailor-made paths to their version of success.

10 Tips for Recruiting and Managing iGens

In summary, iGen employees are creative, independent, and self-directed. They will not necessarily be team players. In their careers, they may have to solve the worst environmental, social, and economic problems in history.

As a review, here are ten tips to help you successfully recruit, engage, motivate and manage your iGen team members.

1. Be clear on your company's mission and values. You must stand for more than the bottom line.
2. Promote your social impact often on social media. The iGen employees you will be recruiting in 10 years will be looking now and then. You must have a strong, and authentic social impact history.
3. Use video and photos to tell your company's story. iGens are visual and will appreciate story-based video, providing it is not overly produced or polished.
4. iGens are willing to work harder than previous generations for advancement.
5. They expect long-term personal and professional development from day one. Start your employee engagement programs immediately.
6. They don't want a "boss," they want a "mentor" they can respect. They are willing to learn so teach them.
7. Like Millennials, they will require constant feedback and encouragement. Schedule weekly feedback conversations in your calendar. You cannot use stone age "annual reviews" for iGens or Millennials
8. They will not necessarily be classic "team players," but they will be good collaborators and will prefer face-to-face communications more than Millennials.

119

9. Because they grew up in unstable, tough economic times, they ranked traditional benefits like salary, health benefits, and retirement plans as top priorities.
10. They are concerned that older generations won't take them seriously. Ask for and recognize their contributions publicly and often.

Section 2

Intergenerational Preferences are Changing and Disrupting Everything

Chapter 8

Media and Entertainment

The Silent Generation started in the mid-1920's. The roaring 20's has been noted by radio historians as the time period in which radio broadcasting began. Pittsburgh's legendary KDKA was the first broadcast radio station in the US. KDKA went live in 1920. By 1922, over 600 radio stations were broadcasting across the US. Similar to the iGen "digital natives," the Silent Generation were "radio natives" and never knew a time without the radio. They can recall the family gathering around the radio every evening to listen to everything from radio plays, mystery serials, soap operas, quiz shows, talent shows, variety hours, and the first sitcoms.

When it came to media consumption, radio ruled until the early 1950's when pictures "flew through the air" right into your home. The "golden age of television" was the 50s and 60s in the Baby Boomer's formative years. Television started out primarily broadcasting live shows until the first video recording device was developed around 1958. For Boomers, they were the "television natives," and never knew a time without both radio and television. They enjoyed television shows in black and white and eventually color, many of which were converted radio shows, like Amos and Andy, Gunsmoke, and Father Knows Best.

What about Gen X, the forgotten generation. Society "forgot" to give us our own new device to call our own but we did see one of the mediums, transform to a clearer more pleasing experience. It was when FM radio started playing our favorite songs, not just classical music.

As a Gen X / Boomer Cusper born in 1965, I was fortunate to grow up around the radio business. My family worked in the radio business, and we had friends that owned local radio stations. As a child, I was the "go to" source for any kid-

124

based sound effects. Back then all sound effects for commercials and programming had to be created on site. There were no digital libraries with every sound known to man and beast. The only way you could make a broken glass sound, was to grab a microphone and break some glass. I was the kid charged with throwing the baseball through the glass and no, I didn't wear safety goggles.

Carl Venters was my father's longtime friend from the University of North Carolina. When I was growing up in Raleigh, NC, Carl was the president and general manager of the area's number one radio station, WPTF-AM. My mom was the promotions director for the station, so I was always hanging out there because I loved the vibe. WPTF had an FM station at the time that played classical music, like most FM stations across the US. AM radio was all the rage at that time, and most of the top stations across the US were AM. Most automobiles didn't even have FM bands on their radios, so FM primarily aired classical music or what I called "elevator music."

Carl, who remains a great friend and mentor, felt there was a better use of FM other than elevator music. One day, his sixteen-year-old son, Lee, came to him with an observation that changed everything. He said, "Dad, have you heard what the college stations are playing? They are playing rock and roll, The Stones, CCR, and even Elton John."

Elton John was considered rock and roll in the 70's. Lee, and most young people of the time, loved rock music. My mom loved it too. One of the benefits of working at a radio station back then was that you had unlimited access to "just released" rock and roll albums from the radio station. I remember my mom playing Led Zeppelin, Fleetwood Mac, and Rolling Stones records on our speakers at home.

In the early seventies, the powerhouse radio stations usually aired local talk radio programs or Top-40 hits. In my hometown, the aforementioned WPTF-AM was number one. They had a great lineup of talk show hosts like Bart Ritner's "Ask Your Neighbor" morning show. A close number two was WKIX-AM 850 where the legendary DJ, Rick Dees started his career. Carl was ready to shake up the Raleigh radio market, so he listened to his son, Lee, and started to develop a radical plan to transform his classical music WPTF-AM to Rock. They called it the "Rock and Roll Revolution." Carl came up with the controversial idea to play rock and roll over the FM frequency for the first time ever.

Carl did some research and learned about Lee Abrams, a 19-year old DJ from Detroit, who had come up with a new rock format called SuperStars. The format played a variety of songs from rock and roll superstar albums, not just the current hits. Carl flew to Detroit a few times to try to convince Abrams to come to Raleigh to help him transform WPTF-FM into a rock and roll powerhouse. At the time, Raleigh was a significantly smaller radio market than Detroit and radio heads typically don't downgrade in market size. Eventually, Abrams surcame to Carl's exciting and disrupting plan.

Carl and Lee set out to start the Rock and Roll Revolution and changed WPTF-FM to WQDR. "QDR" stood for "quadraphonic," meaning playing music out of four speakers. Carl understood that Rock and Roll sounded best in quadraphonic sound, so WQDR was born of that fact.

126

Using the SuperStar format, WQDR would become the first commercial rock-formatted FM station in the nation. The format would later be called AOR, or Album Oriented Rock, a term still used today.

WQDR went on the air the day after Christmas, December 26, 1972, at midnight. The last song on WPTF-FM was "Jingle Bell Rock", while the first on WQDR was "Bitch" by the Rolling Stones. The WPTF-AM staff, and the entire Raleigh community was in shock. News-Talk WPTF-AM employees worked in ties and were very professional. WQDR DJs and staffers came to work in torn jeans, and there were even rumors that there were drugs in the studio during the overnight shifts. When people across Raleigh came back to work after the holidays, they turned on their classical background music in the office and were shocked to hear "Start Me Up" by the Stones instead. There was such outrage, Carl had to go on Ritner's Ask Your Neighbor, explain the change, and take calls from irate WPTF-AM classical fans.

Eventually, Carl was able to smooth out the multi-station relationships and calm down the Raleigh classical music listeners. Within a year, WQDR had double-digit ratings, and the "Superstars" format was being used in over 30 radio markets around the US. Carl went on to own multiple radio stations across the Carolinas. Abrams consulted for hundreds of AOR stations and was an early senior executive at XM Satellite Radio where he programmed all of their radio stations.

So Gen Xers were the "FM Natives." I was only eight years old, and I remember vividly, hanging out with those long-haired hippy rock and roll DJs in the studio, watching them

127

spin their records in awe. This was a defining experience for me and it had a lot to do with me becoming a radio and nightclub DJ as well as a lifelong lover of all things music.

Digital media has changed everything. When Boomers and Xers were in their formative years, their media consumption choice was to either watch TV, listen to the radio, or play albums in their bedrooms. Today, radio and TV are still a solid choice, but they compete with everything from streaming broadcasters, like Pandora and Netflix, to Podcasts. Not to mention that fact that Steve Jobs changed the media landscape when he introduced the media game changer, the iPod.

Most of us remember Job's famous introduction of the iPod in 2001. He said, "The coolest thing about the iPod is that your entire music library fits in your pocket. OK? You can take your whole music library with you, right in your pocket. Never before possible. So that's iPod."

For the remainder of this chapter, I am going to discuss how Millennials and iGens prefer to consume media and entertainment. I will talk about how radio and television are doing with all their new and disruptive competition for eyes and ears. Since I am, and always will be, a broadcast "radio geek," let's start with how radio is doing today.

Radio Today

A lot has changed in the radio world since those days of hanging out with rock and roll DJs at WQDR. I am sure many Gen Xers and Boomers can remember calling your local radio station to request a favorite song. You would sit around for hours, enduring endless commercials and chatty

128

DJs while waiting for your song to play. Today, your favorite song can be accessed from multiple mediums, at the touch of your finger, without commercial interruption.

One would assume that radio today must be suffering, right? Why would anyone listen to commercials if they didn't have to? Just plug in, or Bluetooth your smartphone right through your car speakers... and it is musical bliss. That is the perception, but perception is not reality in this case. In 1973, broadcast radio enjoyed a dominating 90 percent weekly reach in the US. That means nine out of ten people across all generations listened to broadcast radio at least once in a given week. Guess what that reach is today?

According to Nielsen Radio Ratings, in 2017, broadcast radio still has a 90 percent reach. So, what about young people? They certainly must be tuning out. Surprisingly, over 93 percent of Millennials listen to broadcast radio daily.

As a veteran of the early radio days, I could not be happier with these findings; however, like you, I am surprised by these statistics and I wanted to find out why this was the case. I reached out to Gayle Troberman, Chief Marketing Officer at iHeartMedia, the most substantial radio broadcasting company in the U.S.

iHeart has been the beneficiary of another broadcast media trend since my WQDR days, consolidation. In my early days of radio broadcasting and advertising sales, I worked for one station and competed with the other stations in the market. Today, it is not uncommon to find upwards of eight radio stations owned and operated by one broadcasting company. Entercom and iHeart are the biggies.

iHeartMedia owns 855 local broadcast radio stations and reaches 110 million listeners across the U.S. every week. iHeartMedia was rebranded from Clear Channel in 2014 to align with the rapid success of their iHeartRadio online and mobile app. iHeartRadio is a digital service that features live streams from their 850-plus locally owned and operated radio stations, as well as hundreds of others. They also feature thousands of on-demand podcasts and host marquee events like the iHeartRadio Music Festival and the iHeartRadio Music Awards, which had over 165 billion social media impressions in 2016.

Gayle Troberman has been leading marketing efforts at iHeart since 2015 and consulted on the Clear Channel to iHeart name change. She also spent ten years leading marketing initiatives at Microsoft. I asked Gayle how radio was holding its own with all the other music choices Millennials, iGens, and the different generations have with today's technology.

Gayle said, "Broadcast radio is not music. Every generation has had their music collections. For Boomers, it was albums and 8-tracks. Gen X'ers had their cassettes and CDs. Millennials and iGens have their digital music collections, which could include streaming subscriptions. Broadcast radio is more than music. It's live, local conversations with real people." She goes on to say, "For decades, people have had their favorite on-air personalities. They listen to them in the car on the way to work, and they develop a personal connection. Elvis Duran has over 14 million regular listeners."

Elvis Duran is an American radio personality. He is the host of the daily morning radio program "Elvis Duran and the Morning Show" in New York City on iHeartMedia's Z-100.

Gayle said, "Sixty percent of listening happens in the car." I told her about my car and the many options I have for music and entertainment. I have my smartphone that I can Bluetooth. My car has an internal hard drive with more than 2,000 songs. I have Sirius-XM Satellite Radio. I can stream Pandora, iHeartRadio, or even listen to an audiobook on Audible. So why do so many people still listen to broadcast radio in the car? "In a car, you can't read your phone, well, at least you're not supposed to. If you plug into the music library of your choice," Gayle says, "you are fully disconnected. You are alone. That is an uncomfortable place to be, especially for young people."

We then discussed Millennials and iGens specifically. I asked Gayle why they decided to change the name of their company and if it had anything to do with Millennial's and iGen's love of streaming services like iHeartRadio? She answered, "Streaming is here to stay. If anyone is going to disrupt us, it's us." That mindset was the catalyst for creating iHeartRadio. Since iHeartRadio launched in 2008, they have amassed an astounding 100 million registered users. One-third of iHeartMedia's on-air listeners use the iHeartRadio app as well. One of the reasons for the iHeartRadio app's success is that people like to follow their favorite radio stations. If you grew up listening to Elvis Duran in New York City and you move away to go to college in California, you can still listen to Elvis live on your iHeartRadio app.

Another interesting observation from Gayle regarding Millennial and iGen listeners is their ability to seamlessly

131

jump from device to device. "The device is becoming a less important factor in regard to where we consume media. The peak listening time for the iHeartRadio App is from 9:00 to 10:00 AM." This makes sense if you look back to the statistic that shows 60 percent of listening happens in the car. If you are driving to work and you are listening to your favorite morning show, it is possible to become so engaged in the conversation that you don't want to turn it off when you get to the office. We have all been there. Now, you simply turn off the car, throw in your headphones, tap the iHeartRadio app, and you don't miss the show. The same happens if you use the desktop app on your computer at work. 9:00 to 10:00 am is when you seamlessly switch from your car radio to smartphone app to desktop without missing a minute of your favorite morning show.

Broadcast radio is thriving, and companies like iHeartMedia have not fought the inevitable streaming radio disruption, they have adapted and embraced it.

Television Today

The story is not as pretty for broadcast and cable television. While radio has held the same audience reach for the past thirty years, TV has seen as much as a 50 percent decline in viewership in the same period. "Cord cutting," ditching cable, and using only streaming services, is on the cusp of going mainstream. Nielsen found in 2016, broadband-only homes rose 28 percent to nearly 5 million from 3.9 million, in a single year.

It's no surprise that Millennials and iGens are leading the charge when it comes to cord cutting. iGens spend more time online on their smartphones than they do on all other devices combined. As we learned in the iGen chapter, iGen smartphone ownership (96%) dwarfs their ownership of other media devices.

Despite the cord-cutting movement, a Deloitte study found that pay-TV subscriptions, like cable, are holding their own at 74 percent of US households. However, their research noted that two-thirds of pay-TV consumers say they keep their pay-TV subscriptions because it is bundled with their internet.

Fortunately for cable and television broadcasters, TV usage climbs as we get older. With 76.4 million Boomers in the US, many are retiring and grabbing the remotes. TV will be okay for the near future. According to Nielsen, viewers 65 and up watch 51 hours of TV per week. Millennials watch less than half that amount at 22 hours per week, while iGens only watch TV 15 hours per week, an 11 percent decrease year-over-year.

But while time spent viewing traditional TV is decreasing for everyone except seniors, the total time spent on all media reached a new high in 2016, increasing 13 percent from the previous year. In 2016, US adults spent just over 10.5 hours per day consuming media. Cable's survival as a dominant medium lies solely in the hands of older generations. While they are surviving today, cable TV can't fight youthful, disruptive generations forever.

Younger generations are driving the decline in traditional and cable TV viewing by opting for streaming video services like Netflix, Amazon Prime, Hulu, and even YouTube. With many of these services creating their own, high-quality, binge-worthy programming, you can expect the cord-cutting to continue.

Online Video and Streaming Video Services

Millennials, iGens, and to a lesser degree, Gen X'ers are watching less traditional TV, and that is great news for Netflix and other streaming services. Subscriptions for streaming video services have grown by 18 percent in the past four years. Forty-nine percent of households subscribe to services like Netflix, Amazon Prime, and Hulu.

According to Nielsen research, 61 percent of Millennials say Netflix is their first choice for watching TV. Older iGens and the youngest Millennials, aka iGen/Millennial Cuspers (aged 18-24) are the biggest Netflix fans. Their increased viewing trends have paralleled the increase in Netflix stock prices. In 2011, the average 18-to-24-year-old spent about 27 hours per week watching traditional TV. In 2017, the same group is watching closer to only 14 hours of traditional TV. Netflix stock, in the same period, went from $4.17 per share to $143.61. I kick myself every day for not buying Netflix stock when they were only shipping DVDs through the mail.

A study by GlobalWebIndex found that, in North America, 70 percent of iGens watch Netflix. Worldwide, iGens consume Netflix at a rate 25 percent higher than everyone else. iGens watch more online TV than any other generation, averaging 1 hour, 11 minutes per day.

Again, it's no surprise that these digital natives are gravitating toward digital content. The iGens will be even more inclined to go digital, as flipping through hundreds of channels on cable television or satellite TV will seem even more antiquated and arbitrary than it does to older generations.

According to GlobalWebIndex, online video has also become a fully established entertainment platform. Among all internet users, 92 percent watch video clips online, with just under half watching online TV or movies. Regular viewing of online TV jumps to nearly three-quarters (71 percent) for iGens and young Millennials.

Not only do they stream, they stream for long periods of time. Younger audiences love to binge watch their favorite online programs. Deloitte found that 40 percent of iGen and Millennial binge watchers do so weekly. They average a staggering six episodes or five hours of viewing in a typical binge-watching session.

Going to the Movies

One of the common themes at the movie industry's annual conference, CinemaCon, is addressing the issue of decreasing cinema attendance by iGens and Millennials. According to the Motion Picture Association of America, the share of moviegoers aged 18-40 has fallen over the past five years.

Like so many other categories, we see technology as a major contributing factor. Since iGens and Millennials are the most connected to their technology, it is no surprise they are the most significant demographic segment that is choosing to view movies on other devices, as opposed to going to a movie theatre. There are a lot more screen-based entertainment options today. Young people are not as excited about heading to the cinema on the first day a movie

135

is released as older generations may have been. Millennials and iGens are the kings of "instant gratification;" however, they are willing to wait a few months to see new movies at home in the comfort of their rooms. They have enough things to occupy their time during the wait. As you learned earlier, they have Netflix shows to binge on. Millennials are also a nostalgic bunch and will scroll through endless choices of movies on Netflix or Amazon Prime to find classics from their childhood to re-watch again with friends. They also have video games and a continuous stream of social media to keep them occupied.

You must also look at finances when assessing why younger moviegoers are slowing down. Many young people are struggling to pay the bills, so forking out $15 for a single movie ticket, plus a small fortune for popcorn and a soda is not very pragmatic. They can save a lot of money by watching an older movie at home with a group of friends.

Being master multi-taskers, the thought of sitting in a dark theater, uninterrupted for several hours, is not a comfortable experience for young people. The first thing the theater screen tells them to do is to turn off their smartphone, and you know they don't want to do that. At home, they can watch a movie while doing other tasks like "checking in." They can also pause the movie when they need to do something else, like making their own popcorn in the microwave.

Older generations don't go to movies as much either, and this has been the same for decades. They tend to want to stay home and will opt for TV shows or even reading a book. The outlier to this trend is when they are with their kids and grandkids. Parents and grandparents alike still enjoy taking

136

their kids to kid-friendly movies. It is still one of the top entertainment options for parents because it is safe, and it gives them a break. This is one of the reasons you see so many animated movies targeted at children being released these days, especially around holidays and times when kids are not in school. You may also notice that companies like Pixar and Disney go out of their way to creatively inject adult humor into the children's films so that everyone can be entertained.

One of the ways cinema companies are addressing the decline of young moviegoers is to focus on the "experience" as much as they focus on the latest release. Millennials, as you have learned throughout this book, are all about the "experience." New mega-multiplexes are popping up all over the US that offer a full evening of entertainment where the movie is just a part of the overall experience. Most new facilities today include arcades, gaming, and places for people to safely congregate and socialize before and after the movie. Many also offer in-theatre dining options (which works particularly well for young Millennial families who often have to choose between dinner and a movie). Some theatre chains are also adding full bars as well.

As it relates to the "smartphone" issues, some chains are finding ways to engage tech-savvy Millennials and iGens and their devices without sacrificing the general movie-going rules and regulations regarding these distracting devices. Cinemark, for example, is using a dedicated Cinemark app that can be placed in "CineMode" during the movie. They even provide rewards in exchange for the promise to use the app during the movie. Theatres are also making sure they are utilizing the latest technology to attract younger viewers. They can offer new and unique experiences with 3D, 4D, and other enhanced viewing experiences that cannot be accessed at home.

Sports and Live Events

When it comes to media and entertainment throughout the generations, the consistent thing we all seek is a stimulating "experience." We look to our entertainment options as ways to "escape." Professional sports and live concert venues have done a good job embracing the overall fan experience.

iHeartMedia doesn't just play music and entertain you with their on-air personalities, they are using their platforms to bring their listeners closer to the artists. They host the successful annual iHeartRadio Music Festival each year and have smaller events in iHeartRadio studios along with their local radio station personalities. Through the iHeartRadio app, they stream the "last 2 minutes" before an artist goes on the stage, giving their listeners a backstage, personal experience with their favorite artist. Sporting events are doing the same thing. NASCAR offers fans headsets and a race app that puts fans directly in the car with their favorite driver. They can hear the driver's strategies with the pit crew and see the real-time speed and other data from the car during the race.

Twitter and other social media networks have made it possible for fans to follow and engage their favorite athletes and celebrities. Fans can get a real "behind the scenes" look into how famous people live their lives. Celebrities have millions of fans. Now they can post regular updates from their off-stage lives. Fans feel a lot more connected with their favorite celebrities and sports figures than they did when they could only see them perform.

138

In summary, today's fans expect to be more than spectators; they expect to be part of the experience.

Chapter 9

Parenting

One thing all generations have in common is that we were all "parented" at some point in our lives. Some of us were parented longer than others and many argue that you are continually parented until your parent passes away.

I am sure my dad would have concurred with the latter. Until he passed away unexpectedly at the young age of 73, I often went to him for advice on everything from my career decisions to raising my son. He gladly provided his fatherly wisdom, and I listened. Fortunately, my mom still fills that need today.

In this chapter, we will focus on parenting styles, specifically as it relates to getting children to adulthood. Again, some people will question when that exactly happens, so we will just focus on the formative years up to high school graduation. I will also focus on moms as parents more than dads, primarily because moms were mostly responsible for everyday child rearing, up until the Gen X generation, when moms finally joined the dads in the workforce.

However, even when both parents work, moms still do the lion's share of the day-to-day parenting and household management. Millennials are starting to change that trend, as they are less likely to buy into the concept of traditional, gender-specific responsibilities, like their parents and grandparents followed. Millennial dads, if they are in the picture, are taking a much more active role in general child-rearing duties.

Most will agree that a lot has changed through the generations as it relates to parenting styles, and much of it can be attributed to the changing societal norms and, most recently, the internet and smartphones.

To outline some of the radical changes, let's start with some "bad parenting" advice examples. Redbook writer, Charlotte Hilton Andersen, provided a detailed look at the different generations of parents and everyday thoughts that went unchallenged at the time. Feel free to smile if you have heard any of your older relatives or friends say these things.

In the 1920s, it was common for parents to follow the idea that ignoring your child was a way to build good, strong character. Behaviorist John Watson warned Silent Generation parents that holding babies too much would spoil them. He said, "Never hug and kiss them or let them sit in your lap. Shake hands with them in the morning. Pat them on the head if they have made an extraordinarily good job of a difficult task."

Moms in the 1940's were told to "stop coddling their boys." Then as the pendulums tend to swing from one extreme to the next, 1950's mothers were told they needed to "bathe their baby three times per day." In the 1800's mothers were told to roll their babies in lard every day, so this pendulum swung way back. Cleanliness was an ongoing theme in the 50's. Mothers were told never to let anyone kiss their baby, but if it had to happen, to hold their baby, so the kiss lands on the back of the baby's neck. Maybe that had something to do with adolescents in the 50's later rebelling by rolling around in the mud for days at a time at Woodstock.

When to start babies on solid food has been argued about across all generations, and it still debated today. 1960s mothers followed the advice of Dr. Walter Sackett, author of the book "Bringing Up Babies," who advised starting newborns on solid foods at two days old. He further suggested that babies could have vegetables at two weeks

143

old and, by three months, they could eat bacon and eggs. Finally, he said babies could start drinking daily coffee at the ripe age of six months.

Mothers in the 1980's were told: "babies sleep better on their stomachs." This position would keep them from choking if they got sick during the night. Doctors furthered the point by saying "front sleeping" was safest for infants and would also prevent scoliosis, make babies more confident, prevent mental illness, help with colic, and keep them from waking themselves with flailing limbs. Unfortunately, this was later debunked due to a massive rise in Sudden Infant Death Syndrome (SIDS). By 1992, the American Pediatric Association had changed the recommendation to "back sleeping," and SIDS deaths dropped by 50 percent.

1990's parents debated about the proper way to discipline their unruly children. "To Spank or Not to Spank" was a book written by John Rosemond. He not only recommended an initial "pop on the rear," he suggested following up with 30-minutes of confinement, which came to be known as the "time out." He went on to make sure parents locked their disobedient children as young as six years old in the bathroom because, "it's isolated and boring."

As you can see from the competing advice parents followed through the years, there was always a parenting "expert" who knew exactly how you should raise your kids. Those experts usually wrote a book or two, the most famous one, of course, being Dr. Benjamin Spock's book "Baby and Child Care," published in 1946. His advice, religiously followed for decades by some, was dismissed as 'nutty' by others. Controversy has swirled around his ideas since the Silent Generation became parents; however, despite the

144

controversy, today, years after his death in 1998, new parents still follow his advice. They just might not realize they do.

Younger Gen X and Millennial parents also have parent experts to follow. The problem now is that the "experts" number in the thousands, thanks to the internet. Now the constant dilemma for parents is deciding who to believe. If you Google "parenting advice" you will get 52,100,000 results in 0.66 seconds. As parents or caretakers in the new Millennium, we've all been there. You can search for the answer to your child's particular ailment, read one article and the very next article you read will tell you to do the complete opposite. We have gone from not enough information to way too much information. Yet another radical pendulum swing.

More than a million Millennials are becoming moms each year. Most of them will be searching the world-wide-web for answers to everything from when to stop breastfeeding to how to know if my child is suffering from depression?

1.3 Millennial women gave birth for the first time in 2016, according to data released from the National Center for Health Statistics. This raised the total number of U.S. women in this generation who have become mothers to more than 16 million. In total, Millennial women accounted for about nine-in-ten US births in 2016. Over 9,000 Millennial women become new moms every day.

While they now account for the majority of annual US births, as you learned in the Millennial chapter, Millennial women are waiting longer to become parents than past generations. Most credit the reasons for the postponement to: a shift away from marriage, increased educational attainment, and the movement of more women into the labor force. Student debt also has a direct correlation.

Even though Millennials are waiting longer to get married and have children, when they do have kids, they are notably confident about their parenting abilities. A 2015 Pew Research survey found that half of the Millennial parents surveyed (52%) said they are doing a very good job as a parent, compared with 43 percent of Gen X parents and 41 percent of Baby Boomer parents. Millennials not only feel good about their parenting, they seem to be having more fun parenting than older generations. Fifty-eight percent of Millennial parents said parenting is rewarding and enjoyable all the time, where only 39% of Gen X and Baby Boomer parents agree with that statement.

As I mentioned in the introduction, I worked for a children's publishing company that relied on over a million parent volunteers to manage their literacy events in 60,000 schools across the US. In my role; I was responsible for engaging those parent volunteers and helping the schools recruit, inspire, and retain their volunteers. I quickly learned there was a stark contrast to how younger Millennial parents liked to engage with their child's school versus parents from older generations. Like workplaces, schools are experiencing a newfound "age diversity" of parents. More than half of k-12 parents are Millennials, 36 percent are young Gen Xers, and the rest are Baby Boomers who may be taking care of their grandchildren. In addition to the parent "age diversity" in schools, nearly all the new teachers hired today are Millennials. Schools must take into consideration the parenting styles and communication preferences of all their parents and teachers. A one-size-fits-all family engagement strategy is no longer effective.

146

Technology has changed everything in the world of parenting. As a Millennial parent, the internet and parenting apps can be both a blessing and a curse. Millennials have grown up with smartphones and instant answers to any question they can ask, at the touch of a finger. It is no surprise that the smartphone and social media are two of the most significant tools Millennial parents utilize today.

It is ironic that the most socially connected generation in history uses their phones for everything, except talking. Fortunately, Millennials' Boomer and Gen X parents, as well as their teachers, helped them navigate the vast amount of digital information in their formative years. This trend is even stronger now for the iGens with many school systems focusing on teaching critical thinking skills as early as kindergarten. With all the information coming at parents from all directions today, it is essential that they use their critical thinking skills to decipher real vs. fake information, or "fake news."

Since there are "experts" everywhere on every topic, how does a parent know who to believe? Millennials are experts in their own right in identifying those experts. Parents will follow experts online and often learn about them through their peers on social media.

One of those Millennial parenting experts with a strong following is Deborah Gilboa, MD (aka "Dr. G"). Dr. G is a family doctor and mother of 4 boys. Her parenting website, AskDocG.com, blog, and seminars encourage and empower parents to raise children they will respect and admire. Dr. G is the author of multiple books including, "Get the Behavior You Want, Without Being the Parent You Hate!" and, parenting activity books focusing on building her "3R's of

147

Parenting:" Respect, Responsibility, and Resilience. She is also a regular parenting and youth development expert on NBC's Today Show, Fox News and ABC's Good Morning America.

I had the pleasure of sharing the stage with Dr. G at a social media event that hosted about 150 top parenting bloggers. I interviewed Dr. G for this book and asked her how today's Millennial parents are different from parents in past generations. One of the most significant issues Dr. G sees with today's parents is that they falsely equate the happiness of their child with being a successful parent. "If my child is happy, I am a good parent. If my child is not happy, I have failed as a parent." She observes this in her family practice and in schools. "Schools are dealing with parents wanting their kids to be happy all the time; they question everything. A parent's success should not be based solely on whether their child is happy or not; it should be based on whether they are growing and learning."

Another radical differentiator evidenced in today's Millennial parents is their advanced critical thinking skills. Dr. G states "Because Millennials grew up in the golden years of the internet and its vast amount of information, we have trained them to question everything. Millennials are programmed to ask for more information or simply ask why something needs to be done a certain way." Dr. G further advises, "If a Gen X employee or teacher questioned something, they might have been seen as disrespectful. Millennial parents, employees, and teachers will challenge the establishment. It is important that we understand that they are not questioning or doubting us, they are just seeking more information."

"Parents are asking schools to provide differentiated learning experiences for their child. In my family practice, Millennial parents want a collaborative care model. Doctors and teachers must show parents that they share the same goals of raising healthy and successful adults."

Social media has been a major disruptor in the parenting world. The average Millennial mom has over 600 friends in her social media circles, and they communicate 24-7. Like businesses, schools must assign someone to monitor their social media activity. Dr. G says, "Millennial parents are used to getting results instantly and have little patience for long lines or chains of command. If a parent hears of a teacher doing something inappropriate with a student on Saturday, they will go to their social media and ask if anyone else has had a similar experience. By Sunday, hundreds of parents, and possibly local news organizations, are involved in the conversation. By Monday at 8:05 when the school bell rings, hundreds of Millennial parents want blood.

Younger companies are doing a good job following their online presence and, as mentioned in previous chapters, many are responding and using social media to stay connected with their happy and unhappy customers. Older, more established companies are catching up. Schools are historically slow to move on all things "new." It wasn't until recently that school districts started allowing their schools to create social media profiles and pages on Facebook and other sites. It's most likely because Millennial parents are demanding social media access to their child's schools.

Dr. G's children attend a school that pays attention. "My kid's school principal creates Google alerts for the school name and even all of her teachers. She wants to be the first to know

149

if something good or bad comes up regarding her school or staff, so she can get in front of it. She also monitors and joins some of her parent's social media accounts and will attend non-school functions in the community if she sees more than three of her students participating."

Maria Bailey is also a friend, mentor, and expert on Millennial moms. Ad Age called her "One of the must-follow women on social media," and credited her with creating the "Marketing to Moms" niche. Maria is an award-winning author, radio talk show personality, internationally known speaker, and the foremost marketing authority on marketing to moms. Her company, BSM Media is a full-service marketing and media firm that specializes in connecting brands with Millennial mothers. She has worked with over 300 brands across the globe including Walmart, Huggies, HP, Disney Parks, and many more family brands. I interviewed Maria to explore how some of her clients are adapting to fit Millennial moms' needs and find out what parent trends are driving the changes. As I mentioned earlier, more Millennial dads are involved, but Millennial moms still predominantly drive household purchase decisions, so I spoke to Maria specifically about those moms.

Maria notes three primary drivers related to Millennial moms. Those three drivers are:
1. Millennial mom's own mom's influence.
2. Millennial mom's desire for connectedness.
3. Technology is everything with Millennial moms.

Let's take a closer look at those three drivers...

Maria tells me, "Millennial moms like their moms a lot." She goes on to say, "Where Gen Xers grew up independent and aspired to do things differently as parents, Millennials want to raise their children collaboratively with their moms. Millennial moms went shopping with their moms as teens, and they still enjoy calling mom and joining her at the mall to shop today." This trend is bringing back the legacy brands that their moms used. "Millennial moms are comfortable using the brands that their mom used and still endorses today. For today's mom, we see a resurgence from nostalgic brands like Coleman, Crayola, Sesame Street, Coca-Cola, and Huggies."

As we have mentioned many times in this book, Millennials crave experiences. As for Millennial's desire for connectedness, experiences are what connects Millennials to the brands they love. Maria says, "For Millennial moms, the experience is as important as the product or service. It is important for brands to be relevant and that their messaging speaks to the consumer as a mom and doesn't just focus on their product's features and benefits. Moms want to know how the product relates to her and how it will make her life easier. Product messaging must also be authentic. Millennials understand Photoshop and will identify and reject messages that are not real."

"As for technology, Millennial moms were born into it and they have been connected since birth. They rely on technology to manage their schedule and their family. Millennial moms will select family doctors and dentists based on whether the office accepts online or text-based appointments." Boomers and Gen Xers remember the chore chart and the stick-on stars. Millennial parents are using apps like MyJobChart where parents assign chores from their smartphone to their child's phone. Their children complete a chore, and the parent is notified. Once mom checks that the

151

chore has been completed, the child gets allowance through the app and can spend it how they wish.

Millennial moms are also using smartphones to manage their family finances. Maria has a name for them. "The Mom Frugalista seeks coupons and ways for their family to save money. They share their success with other moms to build credibility as a savvy shopper. They use apps like Acorns that rounds up their everyday purchases to the next dollar and sends the spare change to their child's college savings account. They love Target's Cartwheel perks program that gives them savings based on their shopping habits." Target claims on their website that they have helped consumers save over $1.2 billion with the program.

Millennial moms use technology to stay connected with family through social media and by using products from HP. "Millennial parents will buy the new HP printer and send it to their parents. Technology enables them to be at their child's soccer game and send a real-time picture directly to grandma's printer a thousand miles away."

Finally, Millennial moms care about social justice and support brands that align with their values. They support B-corps, a designation that assures companies are giving back to the greater good and producing products in an environmentally sustainable way. Jessica Alba's Honest Brand, Method, and Toms are Millennial mom favorites.

In summary, brands that want to resonate with Millennial parents should focus on moments, emotional connection, nostalgia, social impact, and lifestyle.

So, what will parenting look like in the year 2027? TeenSafe, a website followed by millions of parents that promises to "keep their teen safe," had some thoughts on the future. Most of the future is an extension of what we are starting to see with young Millennial parents today.

They will continue to focus on raising resilient and compassionate children.

Parents will understand the challenges their kids will face getting through school, finding a job, supporting a family, and paying off debt. They will teach their children to overcome obstacles instead of being defeated by them. These children will be aware of the privileges they enjoy as ever-evolving media and technology will enable them to see the real-time tragedies that happen daily across the world. They will be the first to help their neighbor and treat others with kindness and respect. It will be up to Millennial parents to lead by example and show their kids compassion if they want them to grow into compassionate adults.

Technology will continue to make parenting easier.

We have already discussed how Millennial parents are taking full advantage of smartphone apps and online-based parenting experts to become better parents. This will continue to grow and evolve and help even more parents in the future.

Legacy brand, Fisher-Price, recently imagined what parents' lives would look like in the future. The company imagines a world where toys are more interactive, so kids entertain themselves on their own, freeing up more of their parent's time. For example, tomorrow's kids may play in virtual toy

153

rooms, where the artificial intelligence-based toys would respond to how kids want to play at any given time.

Fisher-Price also predicts technology-enabled parenting aids will evolve as well. For example, tomorrow's baby monitor will alert a parent when their child is awake as it does today; however, it will also let the parent know why he is awake. Does he need to be fed? Does he need to be changed? Parents won't have to guess anymore.

Fisher-Price also imagines a world where this type of monitor would be able to determine which parent to wake up based on which stage of the sleep cycle each parent is in at the time. Won't this make shopping for baby showers interesting?

Chapter 10

Education

Education is my sweet spot. I have spent my life working in and around educational systems. Like most of us, I spent twelve years in elementary, middle and high school. These K-12 formative years set us up to become successful adults.

I then spent an additional five years at East Carolina University, where I tweaked and molded my career vision into what ended up keeping me close to schools my whole life.

After spending nearly a decade in radio and the music industry, I landed at Entertainment Publications (EPI). EPI produced the Entertainment Books that K-12 schools and nonprofit organizations used to raise much-needed funds. I used my broadcasting experience to help create a media campaign that promoted the good that was happening in education. The program was called "One for the Community" (OFTC). OFTC ultimately aligned with 125 television stations and 65 professional sports teams to generate excitement around the Entertainment Books. The partners used their airwaves and newscasters to report on the great projects that schools were able to fund with the money they earned from the sale of those books.

By the time I finished my fifteen-year run at EPI, the program had raised more than $90 million annually for schools and nonprofit community organizations. This experience was very rewarding as it addressed two of my core passions; increasing awareness of community and societal issues and then helping schools, students, and their families.

After fifteen years of helping schools address funding challenges, I switched my focus to literacy. I joined forces

156

with the world's largest children's book publisher. Their mission is to help all children become lifelong readers. The challenge is that many schools and communities lack the resources, books, and family support that's needed to meet their mission.

I accepted the challenge and helped create another education-based media awareness and support campaign called "Read and Rise." Read and Rise put books into the hands of underserved students in some of the poorest schools in the nation. The program aligned with hundreds of radio stations, their on-air personalities, and corporate partners like Target, Walmart, and Kellogg's to promote the importance of independent reading. Another goal of the program was to connect kids with books that they actually wanted to read for fun. Read and Rise, and our media partners, had a great run and delivered nearly a half million books to kids in need. The campaign also blasted over $10 million worth of literacy awareness messaging through everybody's favorite radio stations. In the latter half of my decade at the publisher, as you know, I also managed their million-plus volunteer army, mostly comprised of Gen X and Millennial moms.

I share my background with you to demonstrate my knowledge of the K-12 education systems. I have been blessed with the gift of creativity and collaboration. When I am presented with a societal challenge that I am passionate about, I have always found it easy to connect the dots and bring the right people and organizations together to foster and facilitate positive change. Building community collaborations that address local education issues requires a lot of knowledge of how the system works.

157

Before we look at ways to help schools and educational institutions, we must appreciate and accept the fact that these institutions are large, often set in their ways, and have challenges with "new ways of doing things." This is similar to large corporate organizations. They have many layers, they are historically risk-averse, and they can resist change, because change in such a large organization is difficult. It takes someone with in-depth knowledge of the "system" to get things done.

As you have read throughout this book, technology and the younger generations are disrupting everything; so educational institutions are starting to react, by necessity, to the changing needs of iGen students, Millennial teachers, and families. While it is encouraging to hear leading educators pushing change, it is still not happening fast enough in my humble opinion. I am not alone in that assessment. Steve Case, the founder of AOL, in his book "The Third Wave," predicted education would be one of the last industries to adopt "the internet of things." The "internet of things," Case says, is the third wave of the internet where everything is intertwined and managed through the internet. It simply makes things work better, faster, and more efficient.

There are hundreds of "Third Wave" ed-tech startups that are creating amazing internet and app-based technology for schools. Their products address a host of education's most significant challenges. Ed-Tech is being utilized to manage everything from student data to personalized learning. Interestingly enough, there are still a lot of great new tech-tools that are going unused because of the risk-averse nature of the school systems. If their programs do get approved by the school districts, they often get caught up in so much bureaucracy, that the program never makes it to the school or benefits a student. As I said, educational institutions are aware of the challenges they face in a new, faster and hyper-connected world. They will entertain meetings with companies that have tech-based solutions, but unfortunately, in many cases, they still revert back to more traditional models that are comfortable, less risky, and not as efficient.

I have had first-hand experience with this challenge in my educational consulting business. Many of my clients are Ed-Tech companies. They utilize our services to help form alliances in the education space. One of those clients was an adult-targeted telehealth company that provided access to mental health counselors through a mobile device.

You may remember the iGen section where we discussed the silent epidemic of teen mental health. Mental health is one of the education system's most pressing challenges. According to the National Institute of Health, eighty percent of US teens have admitted to suffering from anxiety or depression in the past year. Teen suicides are up over 300 percent since 2012. Although the American School Counselors Association recommends a 250 to 1 student counselor ratio, the national average for the 2014- 2015 school year was 482 to 1. If the 80 percent figure is accurate, how can one high school counselor manage 385 students with mental health issues? The mental health problem is more severe on college campuses where the student to counselor ratio averages around 800 to 1. Students often must wait weeks just for an initial intake exam to review their symptoms.

High school counselors are doing all that they can with their 400-plus students. They are asked to do much more than

159

counsel students on their emotional health; they also manage standardized testing, college admissions, applications, and more. An ever-increasing number of anxious and depressed iGen students need a professional to talk to, but there are clearly not enough ears to go around.

Our company worked with the adult telehealth company to develop a teen version of their platform. The teen version provides teens with 24/7 access to a licensed counselor. The best thing about the program is that it could be accessed through the student's smartphone, where they live every minute of their waking lives. As you know, young people are used to getting instant gratification. When they are stressed or anxious, they want to talk to someone now, not weeks later. It made perfect sense to me that this technology was a solution that could provide teens a professional to talk to when they needed it, where they needed it, and in a format that they are very comfortable with - texting on their smartphones.

To launch the program, the company asked us to find some school districts that would like to offer the service at no charge for six months to all their teen students. We identified the school districts from close contacts and even from Google searches that quickly pulled up news articles about mental health and even suicide epidemics in the school district. After six months of calling hundreds of school districts, I only found one that was willing to give it a try, and they refused to endorse or promote it broadly to the parents or students as an available option, so it was not successful.

Most of the school districts took my calls and meetings but eventually went into risk-averse mode, asking, "What if a student uses the service and they commit suicide?" My answer was always, "What if they don't use it and commit suicide'?"

Ultimately, most of the districts decided to address the mental health challenges of their students by securing funding to hire more counselors. This is what they have done in the past, so it was a comfortable decision. Now the counselor may only have 300 students to manage.

Fortunately, our hard work in helping develop the service was not done in vain. The company will be making it available for parents and teens soon. Parents will have to find it themselves as they most likely won't be hearing about it from their child's school. If you are a parent with a teen who can benefit from anytime, anywhere smartphone access to a professional counselor, please Google "telehealth counseling" to learn more and find resources. I believe this technology can be a lifesaver.

I bring up these challenges because I want to make sure you understand the issues that schools and many larger organizations face. Many employees in the schools, including Millennial teachers, want to change things, but get frustrated with the pace. Most teachers and parents in K-12 schools are Millennials. Some research shows that as many as fifty percent of new Millennial teachers leave the profession within five years, so it is obvious their needs are not being met.

For the rest of this chapter, we will discuss how K-12 schools can meet the needs of this unique generational dynamic as they are very different than past generations. We will also look at the iGens and how they are affecting the way colleges recruit and engage them as the traditional recruitment and application process is being challenged.

Millennial Teachers

I want to start by sharing my admiration for the teaching profession. In my 25 years of working in and around schools, I have developed friendships with thousands of dedicated teachers. Some have even brought me to tears as I watched them engage and inspire their kids. I am so proud of my Millennial/iGen son who is a few years away from completing his teaching degree, and he has chosen to work with high school special needs students. Most of us, me included, can think back to our k-12 years and identify "that special teacher," the one that had a lot to do with you becoming the person you are today. For me, that teacher was Mrs. Jan Lapp, my 11th grade English teacher. Thirty years after my high school graduation, we still keep in touch.

In my career, I have met a lot of teachers - young, old, happy, grumpy, friendly, and mean. One observation has been consistent. Nearly all of them started out their teaching profession with a lot of passion and pride; however, passion can fade through the years if they become frustrated, discouraged, or stagnant. I cannot count the number of times a teacher has said to me, "I wish I could just do what they hired me to do, TEACH!"

If you have learned anything thus far, it is that Millennials are unique. They are unattached, connected, unconstrained, and idealistic. Nearly all new K-12 teachers are Millennials, and they bring these characteristics into the school building. These teachers pose a significant challenge for school leadership.

162

A recent Gallup study of 1,733 public school super-intendents found that just 6 percent of these district leaders strongly agree that their school district understands the needs of Millennials in the workplace. It is imperative that district leaders are aware of what it takes to ensure their new Millennial teachers and all district employees, are set up for success from the start. Whether you are hiring new Millennial teachers, cafeteria workers, or ESE specialists, you must adapt your leadership styles to address these key Millennial worker characteristics.

Millennial teachers are unattached. They are less likely to be affiliated with traditional institutions, such as political parties or religious organizations. Younger teachers may not be as interested in joining teacher unions as their older counterparts.

They are also connected. Millennials grew up with technology. They use it in every part of their personal and professional lives. Millennial teachers do not feel constrained by traditional norms and they reject the adage, "That's the way it has always been done." I know that phrase is said a lot in the education world, but if you tell them that, they may tell you "goodbye." Millennial teachers will push for change in the way things have "always been done." They also see their teaching career and their personal life being more closely intertwined than older generations of teachers did. They seek leaders who care about them as not only teachers, but as people as well.

Finally, Millennial teachers are idealistic, and this will be very good for the teaching industry in the future. Millennials are optimistic, and they search for work that fuels their sense of purpose and makes them feel important. Teaching is, at

163

its core, all about purpose. Nothing makes a teacher feel better about themselves than seeing a student grow and develop. If the school leader does not nurture and recognize their passion, Millennial teachers will switch schools, or maybe even leave the profession for something that is better aligned with their personal growth goals. For Millennial teachers, it's "purpose before paycheck."

School leadership is changing. To recruit, inspire, and retain Millennial teachers, school leaders should adapt and adhere to six key workplace changes, which are identified by the Gallup educator survey.

Purpose: As mentioned before, Millennial teachers do not seek work solely to pay the bills, they seek meaningful work that fuels their sense of purpose. Based on what US teachers earn, I would guess that this is a trait inherent in most teachers.

Personal and Professional Development: Schools spend a lot of money on personal development (PD), and most teachers are required to continue their professional development to earn CE (continuing education) credits. Don't fall prey to the Millennial workplace stereotype that tries to satisfy Millennial workers with a variety of perks. The workplace of the future is moving away from this simple attempt to "satisfy" workers. Smart organizations are prioritizing opportunities for their employees to learn and grow both professionally and personally. Think beyond PD that just benefits the school and think about PD that can help them on a personal level. Consider life skills training, like time and stress management, in addition to the standard work-based professional development.

Millennials want a coach, not a boss. This is a difficult concept in older, established businesses and schools. There is still a very clear ladder, and teachers know which rung they are on. Many still fear having to go to the principal's office. Millennial workers want to be part of a team led by coaches who guide and partner with them to achieve professional and personal goals.

Provide ongoing feedback and conversations. Annual teaching assessments will not work with Millennial teachers. Millennials require real-time continuous communication and feedback. Principals who oversee forty or more teachers will need to rely on team leaders that can make sure Millennial teachers are receiving the timely feedback they crave.

School leaders must focus on Millennial employees' strengths, not weaknesses. Don't get me wrong, shortcomings should be addressed, but must contain a clear growth and development plan. The Millennial teacher thrives when school leaders build on their employees' strengths.

For Millennials, teaching is their life. The schoolhouse of the future will be made up of teachers who are seeking to align their identities and lifestyles with schools and leaders that help them maximize their contribution and thrive at work, and in life.

Gallup provides this simple visual that compares leadership of the past and the future.

PAST	FUTURE
My Paycheck	My Purpose
My Satisfaction	My Development
My Boss	My Coach
My Annual Review	My Ongoing Conversations
My Weaknesses	My Strengths
My Job	My Life

Not many of the nation's superintendents feel confident that their school district is prepared for the onslaught of Millennial teachers and employees today. School leaders need to better understand the changes and communicate transparently with their teams to ensure their school is a great place to work. Leaders also need to focus on making a difference in the lives of the students and families they serve.

Millennial Parents & Family Involvement

As you learned in the previous parenting chapter, 9,000 Millennials are becoming moms every day. They will comprise the majority of K-12 parents by 2025. How can educators prepare for the rise in Millennial parents?

All generations of parents wanted the best for their children, yet they interacted with their child's school differently. Boomer parents were all about independence and would shove their kids on the bus, smile, and wave. For the most part, they were passive observers in the way their child was educated, and they trusted the school to teach their children. Gen X and Millennial parents, who make up the majority of K-12 parents today, play a much more involved role.

Some Gen X parents have been called "helicopter parents" (see Millennial Chapter), as they hovered over their

166

Millennial children, attending to their every need. Other Gen X parents took more of a hands-off approach. Millennial parents are "all in," and they expect to be involved in every aspect of their child's education. They are on a first-name basis with their child's teacher and principal, and they most likely follow the teacher on Facebook and Instagram. Leading parent and child development expert, Dr. G, says schools are up against three things related to Millennial parents.

"First, if their child is not happy, Millennial parents take it personally and consider it a parenting "fail." They will not hesitate to request a teacher change at the slightest hint of their child's unhappiness in class. Second, Millennial Parents want to lead their child's education. They question everything. They will research lesson plans and school policies and challenge the schools by always questioning the source. Finally, Millennial parents engage with the school differently. They follow the school, teachers, and other parents through social media. If anything is suspicious, they will voice their observations and opinions online and on social media. They no longer have to wait until the holiday play to speak with other parents. They do it instantly and often.

While everyone parents differently, there is one thing that Millennials share in common as parents. They believe in the power of technology to maximize their children's education. Millennial parents are the first generation to grow up in a connected world. They are comfortable navigating websites, videos, eBooks, blogs, peer reviews, and social media. They not only know where to find information to help them make decisions, but they also crave it.

Older generations of parents had to go to the school or to the library to access most educational materials and resources. There was a clear separation between school and home. Today's parents have access to anything and everything that's ever been published, right on their smartphones. They also have a massive selection of mobile apps that can help their children learn.

Millennial parents feel empowered to use technology to help their children become better students at home. While the wealth of educational resources at home can help parents, it can also make things difficult for teachers. The days of "the teacher is always right" are over. Millennial parents are not willing to accept what teachers say at face value, and now they have the resources that allow them to "question the source." It is important for teachers to provide constant feedback to Millennial parents on their child's progress and challenges and involve the parent in the education process.

Technology has also changed the way parents communicate with educators. Past generations of parents knew that every Tuesday was "backpack day." That was the day the teacher sent home the "folder" that included things the parent needed to see or sign. As a parent, you better check that backpack on Tuesday, or your child may "miss out." Most schools now utilize online student management platforms like Skyward. Teachers upload their students' data, and parents can log in at any time and see what's going on. Students also use these platforms to get homework assignments, upload homework, and check their grades.

As you learned in the parenting chapter, Millennial moms are super busy, and they use their smartphones for everything, except talking. Calling someone requires an

168

unknown commitment of time that could disrupt their incredibly busy scheduled day. For eons, the epicenter of the school was "the front office." To a degree, that is still the case. When our son was in elementary school, any time we wanted something from the school, it required visiting the front office.

Millennial parents hate the front office. It is a major thorn in their side, yet most schools still require the visit in order to complete most tasks that Millennials feel could easily be completed by text or through an app. One of the main reasons Millennial parents hate the front office is they dread the long waits for everything, especially during the "organized chaos," known as the drop-off or pick up. Millennial parents are accustomed to everything being available on-demand. They avoid long lines at all costs. Schools should aspire to do everything they can to make the Millennial parents' lives easier. They should use technology options as often as possible. Nothing makes a Millennial mom or dad more frustrated than waiting in a long line to sign a piece of paper, drop off a check, or register for the bake sale.

Millennial parents are busier than ever, so what is the best way to get them involved? Since 1897, the Parent Teacher Association, or PTA, was the link between parents and the school. There were usually three-to-four PTA moms or dads that were tasked with fundraising and getting parents "involved." Fortunately for busy parents, they now have access to hundreds of parents and their parent peers through social media, and they don't even have to talk to them. Millennial parents can communicate directly with their child's teacher or principal electronically through Skyward, email, text, and even Twitter and Facebook. This instant access to information that was once provided by the PTA has caused memberships to steadily decline over the past decade.

Schools have always held their traditional family events throughout the year. Most parents attend "Meet the Teacher Night" at the beginning of the year. There is usually a holiday play or event and a few book fairs throughout the year as well. Even those mainstay family events are experiencing a decline in parent participation. The main reasons for the decline are that both parents are working, and they have on-demand access to school information, which was traditionally disseminated at the family events, but is now readily available online.

Schools have done a decent job adjusting to the dual income family challenge, but they can do better. Just because a school has predominantly dual working parents, doesn't necessarily mean a 7:30 am parent event will work. You have to look at the dual working parent dynamic, which could be very different than the early years of two working parents, such as when the Boomer moms entered the workforce in massive numbers in the 70s.

Working arrangements can vary tremendously with Millennial parents. Millennials no longer work nine-to-five. Sorry, Dolly. As you learned in the Millennial chapter, Millennials are always on, and they can be very productive outside the four walls of an office, even in the carpool line. It is not uncommon to see a Millennial parent turn it off at 4:00, take her kids to soccer practice, arrange dinner, bathe them, and put them to bed by nine. Then, they grab a glass of wine and turn it back on, checking and sending emails through their smartphones until midnight. Parents may also travel for their work. The best way to engage Millennial parents is to involve them in the process. Sound familiar?

Every school should start the school year by sending a mobile-based survey to all their parents, asking questions like... What is your preferred method of communication? And, when is the most convenient time of the day (or night) for you to visit the school? Schools should use mobile-based surveys often. You can no longer rely on three parents from the PTA to schedule everything for all the parents. Millennial parents want to be involved in all decisions at school, especially as they relate to their child or their precious time.

Speaking of Millennial parent's time, once you do schedule a family event, make sure you respect their time. Start on time. Have an engaging speaker with interactive, activity-rich content. You only get one shot with Millennial parents. If they take the time to come to a school event and spend the entire time disengaged, head-down in their smartphones, they won't return.

iGens and College Recruitment

The oldest of the iGens are in college and already nearing graduation. They will be entering the workforce soon. For decades, university marketing and admissions departments have used the same formula to recruit students. Those days are changing. Let's look at how iGens are changing the way colleges and universities attract new students.

If you have had a child go to college, you most likely participated in a few college campus visits or tours. The model hasn't changed in decades. You throw your son or daughter in the car. They ride in the back seat for hours, head down, earbuds in, totally tuned out. The end of absence. Look, kids, the largest ball of yarn! No response. Then they finally look up and... voila, "we're here."

You arrive at the campus (that may cost $50 thousand a year for the next four or five years) and get in line. The groans commence from your future scholar. "Sign in please." The tour starts in a large auditorium with several dozen other excited parents and their teens, head down, tuned out. You sit through an excruciatingly long PowerPoint presentation that attempts to sell you on all the great things about their university. Now, remember, iGens have an 8-second attention span, so they sit there, head down, tuned out while parents try to stay awake and set a good example. There are always a few slides which show the "average" SAT scores and GPA from last year's class. Oh *@&#, that's a lot higher than my kid's scores.

After the drawn out, death by PowerPoint slideshow, they wrap up with a cheesy promotional video featuring smiling co-eds, sitting together in a courtyard, chillin on campus, but with no phones or earbuds? Is this reality?

The tour commences with you being paired up with an unnaturally enthusiastic student that never had a bad day in his life. He leads you around campus, parents up front asking questions, teens pulling up the rear, heads down, tuned out. Probably Snapchatting how "lame" the tour guide is.

With younger, more tech-savvy Gen X parents and iGen students, each with the attention span of a goldfish, colleges are finally changing the way they recruit and highlight their universities to potential students and their parents. Parents

172

are still the primary decision makers when it comes to their child's ultimate decision on where to go to college. They have to balance the costs and benefits as well as their child's preferences.

Today's Gen X parents are very different from the Boomer parents of the past few decades. Boomer parents were interested in the amenities and were impressed with things that were not available to them when they went to college in the 70s and 80s. Gen X parents are more cynical. Some are even starting to question the ROI of a very expensive four-year college education. Admissions professionals should address their cynicism head on by creating messaging that highlights the tangible benefits of their school. Instead of focusing on the average GPA of recent applicants, get specific about the percentage of students who secure jobs in their field after graduation.

Once you get Gen X parents on board, the good news is that iGens are more excited than ever about furthering their education. They see value in a college education, but they are also doing a cost-benefit analysis to determine if what they pay is worth the investment. A Northeastern University study found that 67 percent of iGen students indicate that their top concern is being able to afford college. College graduates of the class of 2015 had the largest student loan debt in history. These graduates averaged $30,100 in student debt, up four percent from 2014. Depending on the school, some graduates owed up to $53,000 or more.

The study also revealed that iGens are entrepreneurial and are interested in learning practical skills. Sixty-three percent believe it is important for universities to teach entrepreneurship and 85 percent believe they should be taught financial literacy in college. Forty-two percent expect to work for themselves at some point in their career. This is four times the percentage of Americans who are already self-employed today.

If you are a college admissions professional or a high school counselor, I highly recommend you pick up Corey Seemiller and Meghan Grace's book, "Generation Z Goes to College." Seemiller is a Gen Z (or iGen) expert and a professor at Wright State University. He has some great insight into what colleges need to keep in mind as Gen Z goes to college.

When communicating with future iGen applicants, colleges should throw out most of the Millennial student recruitment playbook. While younger Millennials started to shun polished marketing approaches from traditional retailers, they still responded to slick marketing pieces that they received in the mailbox or their high school guidance counselor's office from universities. They also responded to email. For iGens, email is their least favorite form of communications. They think email is for grown-ups and, as you learned in the iGen chapter, they are in no hurry to be grown-ups. With that said, email is still the most preferred communication tool for their Gen X parents.

Believe it or not, Seemiller found that iGens respond best to face-to-face communications. Seemiller said, "I think in a world where we envision Generation Z as digital natives, we also envision them only being digitally competent and only preferring digital methods of communication. But in many communications, they still like a personal touch. So, as colleges think about recruitment, remember that the face-to-face thing is still very important to them and is probably more important than people are giving it credit."

174

It is no surprise that social media marketing is a must in communication with iGens. However, when it comes to social media, not all platforms are alike. Millennials launched Facebook, and most still use it daily. Most iGens have abandoned Facebook because that is where the adults are. You can still use Facebook to market to Gen X parents, but iGens prefer Snapchat and Instagram, primarily because they love visuals in the form of photos, videos, and stories. iGens don't want to read anything on their devices, they prefer to watch or listen. Short video content that runs anywhere from a minute to no more than 90 seconds works very well with iGens. Schools should take advantage of that by creating short and compelling video content on a regular basis.

Some schools, like Goucher College in Baltimore, are catching on and using the power of video to differentiate themselves. Goucher College and other forward-thinking universities are allowing prospective students to submit video applications instead of written essays. This gives creative, digitally native iGen students an opportunity to showcase their personality as well as their originality.

Like Millennials, iGens require transparency and will reject any messaging that is overproduced or not authentic. A marketing trend that is used with prospective students is allowing them to shadow current students at a school. It is called "virtual following." It gives them the opportunity to hear from real students, not slick and polished marketing, which they despise.

Finally, as we mentioned in the iGen chapter, teens feel they can change the world. This generation does not separate their work from their social outreach. This is a significant change from the previous generation. It is true that Millennials were the first generation that was required to perform community service as part of their graduation requirements. Millennials are also very socially conscious. The difference is that Millennials will have a nine-to-five job and volunteer after work and on weekends. Or, they may take a leave of absence from work to go on an outreach mission. iGens expect their ability to change the world to be ingrained in their everyday job.

Colleges must understand that iGens are hoping to be trained on how to change the world, not just making money. We already discussed iGen's entrepreneurial ambitions. It would be smart for colleges to offer social entrepreneurship, social enterprise, and innovation labs as part of the overall college experience. These should be the first thing they hear about on that college tour as well.

Chapter 11

The Food Industry

Getting together with friends over a nice glass of wine and dinner has been a mainstay for centuries. Most everyone from any generation wants to enjoy good food and drink. Through the ages, what we eat and drink, where we eat and drink, and how that food gets to our plate has changed based on many external factors.

Without a doubt, technology has played an enormous role in changing the relationship we have with food. The internet provides unlimited information on what and where we eat. There are no unanswered questions. With the tap of your finger, you can now access any meal's ingredients, where it was sourced, and how it got to your plate. Technology has also introduced the world to a variety of 'foodie' content through the web, television shows, and online apps. There are even dedicated networks like The Food Network where you can learn about food 24-7. This wealth of information has elevated people from casual diners to restaurant critics, without having years of culinary training.

When looking at each generation's relationship with food and beverages, we aren't that different in our overall likes and dislikes. Some of the most substantial trends in food preparation and distribution are appealing to everyone. For example, everyone still likes a good dining experience and excellent service at their favorite restaurant. The trend in healthier food options has been equally driven both by aging Baby Boomers and the Millennials. Baby Boomers, who are starting to pay more attention to their health and what they put into their bodies, are demanding healthier options and smaller portion sizes; while Millennial healthy options may be driven by local sustainable food sources. Like many industries today, Millennials set the tone and the trends that eventually apply to all generations.

In this chapter, we will compare Boomers and Millennials with the understanding that Gen Xers and iGens are similar in their tastes. We will explore food sources like grocery stores and restaurants. We will also look at the types of foods as well as the way food gets to our plates. Let's start with how Millennials and Boomers approach grocery shopping today.

As I discussed in previous chapters, the grocery store has changed dramatically over the past fifty years. Many Traditionalists and Baby Boomers may remember the "local grocer." They may have even known the butcher by name.

Grocery stores were a lot smaller in the 60s and 70s, yet they seemed to have everything you needed. Gen X came around and started to demand customization and choices. Potato chips that once occupied a small fraction of shelf space on one side of a grocery store aisle, now require both sides of an entire aisle. Today's supermarket aisles are also about three times longer than the grocery store aisles of the 1960s. These days, it seems there are a dozen or more varieties of nearly every type of product. Abundant selection and choice required grocers to build massive stores and even launch "superstores" where you can buy food and tires in the same place.

Boomers are okay with that and are more likely to shop at traditional grocery stores. They are also set in their ways when it comes to brands and will seek out established national grocery store chains to do their shopping. Price is less important than convenience and familiarity to Boomers. It is not uncommon to see older Gen Xers or Baby Boomers shopping at the same grocery store for most of their lives. Grocers are aware of this and have developed some sneaky tricks to disrupt their loyal customers' shopping experience. Every brand strives for customer loyalty, but for grocers, that can hurt the bottom line.

If you are a frequent visitor to a grocery store, you know they are laid out like a grid. You walk in and, in most cases, you turn right. That is by design. It's a well-known fact in the retail community that in North America, 90 percent of consumers, upon entering a store, will turn right unconsciously. The first wall they see is often referred to as a "power wall," and acts as a high-impact first impression vehicle to move product. Grocers often receive big money from brands to place their product displays immediately to the right of the front door. They will also use that first impression space to move product that may be "on the way out." I never grab the strawberries from that cooler at the front door. Beware of perishable foods in the front right entrance of your local supermarket.

Most grocery stores have the fresh and perishable foods around the perimeter of the store like the deli, produce, and meat. The processed, frozen, and packaged foods are in the middle aisles. A good way to shop healthy is to shop the outside perimeter, not the aisles, but that will cost you, as eating healthy can be expensive.

When you grocery shop in the same store all of the time, you subconsciously memorize the layout. My wife, who does most of the grocery shopping for our family, has her list and can get in and out of the store in record time. If I had the same list, it could take me twice as long. This is a problem for grocers, because when you wander around looking for something specific, you buy more. If you know exactly where everything is, you grab what's on your list, and that's it. An extra two or three items per cart can add up to millions of incremental sales for a large grocer.

Have you ever gone to the grocery store for a specific item and go to the spot where it usually is, but it is not there? You say to yourself, "I know this is where the flour used to be." You are not losing your mind. Grocery stores will often move things around and, in some cases, they will do annual redesigns to keep their customers confused. They need us to wonder and wander.

Millennials are not as loyal to one brand or location. They are comfortable shopping for groceries online and often shop at multiple venues, rather than shopping at the one-stop-shop supermarket. Millennials, as you have learned, are more price-conscious. They prefer less expensive foods. They prioritize convenience; however, they are willing to pay a little more for fresh, healthy foods. As a rule, Millennials buy and eat fresh produce more often than older generations.

Millennial's desire for fresh and convenient foods brought about brands like Fresh Market and Whole Foods. These upscale neighborhood markets feature food items Millennials want, like organic and locally sourced produce. They include all the "free" foods like antibiotic-free meats, free range chicken, and an entire aisle of gluten-free offerings. They also cater to busy Millennial's need for convenience by offering healthy, pre-prepared meals that they can throw in the microwave or oven. Many of the stores also have a restaurant featuring hot foods and their deli can provide custom ordered gourmet sandwiches that you can take home or eat in the store. Some people refer to these stores as "groceraunts." Of course, the freshness and convenience come at a price. Many have referred to Whole Foods as "Whole Paycheck."

Whole Foods, Fresh Market, and other groceraunts are experiencing tremendous growth across the US, and they will continue to evolve to meet Millennial and Millennial parent's needs. Amazon is the number one Millennial brand. It is not surprising that they purchased Whole Foods. One can only imagine what those two Millennial brand favorites will be able to develop together. We will have to wait and see.

Both Baby Boomers and Millennials like to eat out. How do restaurants cater to both generation's dining out preferences? It's not as challenging as you may think.

Like their supermarket preference, Boomers are more comfortable with well-known restaurants and tend to favor American, Italian, Mexican, and Chinese restaurants. Boomers are less likely to try Thai, Cuban, or other ethnic options. Millennials, on the other hand, will continually seek out new, unique, and fresh experiences when they dine out. Since many Millennials are straddled with college debt, they are actively trying to save on food. They are eating at home more. They are more prone to order takeout, so they don't have to tip. Every bit helps. Millennials have also brought back coupons in a big way.

Recent research from PRRI-US Consumer Surveys shows that Millennials are using coupons more than their parents, but they are not getting them from any one source and they favor online coupons over paper coupons. Online coupon usage among Millennials has risen 48% over the past two years. The number of Millennials who reported using mobile coupons when dining out rose to 33%, outstripping other generations by a large margin. Another survey by Valassis found that 92% of Millennials use coupons. In the past year, 51% of Millennials said they are using more coupons than the previous year, which is more than Generation X and Baby Boomers.

Millennial parents are using coupons even more. This trend explains the recent growth of companies that offer discounts and coupons like Binghamton-based SaveAround. SaveAround has been around for fifteen years and offers coupon books in more than 170 markets. They also offer an app that gives Millennial parents access to mobile coupons all over the US. Another reason that SaveAround is experiencing growth is the fact that the books help schools and nonprofit community organizations fundraise. Fifty percent of the sale price benefits the selling organizations. This model addresses two strong Millennial values. First, they are "savings savvy" and second, they want to support socially conscious organizations. The SaveAround Coupon Books allow Millennials to save and serve at the same time. It's like "Coupons that Care." I like that.

Millennials lean on their smartphones for everyday purchase decisions, and that includes where to eat. To appeal to Millennials, restaurants must be technologically connected. They should have active social media accounts that feature pictures and information about their menu items. It is critically important for restaurants to manage their reputations on peer review sites like Yelp, TripAdvisor, and others. Millennials are adventurous and are intrigued by food venues and menu items with a story. Since many Millennials have no disposable income for world travel, they are using food and beverage as a way to explore cultures. Millennials are also communal by nature and view eating as a social event. Millennial favorites (like Chipotle) offer larger tables where more people can eat together.

Millennials also seek out locally grown and healthy menu items. With their smartphones, it is easy for them to estimate the carbon footprint of their meal, based on where it comes from. The average restaurant menu ingredient in most American restaurants travels more than 1,500 miles to your plate. This is not cool for Millennials and iGens. This is one reason that farm-to-table restaurants are one of the fastest growing dining segments. Young Americans want healthy food choices, and they want it to be affordable. Healthy and tasty foods that are reasonably priced are now taking precedence over "all-you-can-eat" and "super-sized." Finally, it is important to offer convenience. Millennials and Millennial parents are super busy and always on the run. They prefer fast, delivery, deli foods over casual and fine dining.

Speaking of restaurant delivery, Millennials are changing that too. For Boomers and Gen Xers, ordering food for delivery or takeout is typically limited to pizza or Chinese food. Millennials want more healthy options and more variety. Ninety percent of all restaurant delivery is still in traditional categories like pizza. The local mom and pop restaurants that offer the kinds of food Millennials crave often cannot support delivery. This has given rise to online and mobile app delivery companies that can deliver meals from hundreds of restaurants in a given area.

Millennial foodies have provided internet-based delivery platforms tremendous opportunities for growth. There are five of them that are valued at over one billion dollars. There

184

are two kinds of online delivery platforms. Aggregators (like Grub Hub) offer online portals with a lot of restaurants. Their portal and mobile apps feature full menus and peer reviews. They manage all the ordering, and the restaurant delivers the meals. New delivery services like OrderUp and Bite Squad offer the same features, but also handle the delivery as well.

In addition to delivery, mobile apps have also disrupted the way you search and review restaurants. Baby Boomers grew up in a time where the local newspaper most likely had a popular "food critic." That dude never paid for a meal. Mobile apps (like Yelp) enable everyday foodies to become food critics themselves. Yelp and other peer review systems (like TripAdvisor and OpenTable) are popular with Millennials and other smartphone-enabled diners.

Yelp started in 2004 and features more than 50 million businesses worldwide, providing anyone who has access to the internet the chance to be a food critic. The San Francisco-based company reported having more than 135 million unique visitors in 2014 and more than 71 million reviews on the site.

Restaurant.com says that as many as 82 percent of Millennials will research Yelp before selecting a place to dine out. That percentage grows if they travel outside of their home city. I am a big fan of Yelp and other business review sites. As a business owner, it gives you the opportunity to utilize positive reviews in your advertising. When a business receives negative reviews, it gives the business the opportunity to learn what could be better and to address the issues right on the site, for everyone to see. Transparency is king with Millennials and iGens. It is vital that restaurants

185

constantly monitor their business's Yelp and other online review sites and immediately address both positive and negative reviews on the forum.

There is little doubt that Millennials have impacted the way the food industry sources, manufactures, prepares, and delivers its products. As a whole, the food industry appears to be listening. You definitely see more focus on organic foods, antibiotic-free meat and poultry, sustainable farming, and more transparency. There is even more emphasis on how animals are treated in the food industry. It is important that the food industry continues this trend toward healthier and more sustainable foods. As the Boomers age, Millennials will represent a larger percentage of consumers. It doesn't stop with the Millennials either. The iGens are right behind them. Their generation will be larger and even more concerned with the food they are putting into their bodies.

Chapter 12

Real Estate

Most of the categories we are discussing have a lot of Millennial triggered disruption. The real estate market is experiencing disruption from the older and the younger generations.

First, we will discuss the more pressing issue affecting Baby Boomers and that is the looming senior housing divide. The divide has a trickle-down effect that is making it difficult for Millennials to find their starter homes (which we will touch on in a moment).

Developers, realtors, and other industries are calling it "the Silver Tsunami." In the 70s, the average age in the US was 28. Today, it is 37. According to a 2016 report by the Harvard Joint Center for Housing Studies, the number of Americans over 80 will double in the next two decades - from six million to 12 million. One out of three US households will be headed by someone over 65 by the year 2035. That is close to 79 million Americans, many on the verge of or already in retirement.

Today's retirees are thinking about housing differently than their parents did. When the Silent Generation aged, they typically downsized. As they grew older, they no longer needed the four-bedroom home that they raised their kids in. Even though most of them owned their homes outright, managing the maintenance and hassles of owning a large home became more difficult and less desirable. They cashed out and moved into a smaller house or a condo where there was less maintenance and responsibility. As they got older and into their 80s, many seniors moved into "senior homes," where all their needs are met, including an on-sight medical staff, prepared meals, and nightly activities with their senior home neighbors.

Today's retiree preferences are dividing the senior residential market into two segments. The first is for those 60-to-80 years old, as we discussed in the Baby Boomer chapter of this book. They are seeking "active lifestyle" options. Their desire to stay active and "young" has fueled massive growth in large-scale active living communities, like the Villages in Florida, and themed retirement communities like Jimmy Buffett's Latitudes. These places aren't exactly selling a quiet, relaxed suburban lifestyle.

The second segment is today's Silent Generation and the older Baby Boomers (over the age of 80). These "Octogenarians" are seeking more convenience and a comfortable place to live, with a lot of amenities that make them feel at home.

The challenge to both scenarios is the fact that housing prices have skyrocketed since the record lows during the burst of the housing bubble and the Great Recession. House prices have completely recovered from the 2008 meltdown and now have eclipsed their pre-recession all-time highs. When the Boomers near retirement and start considering downsizing, they are finding that the small homes that were once a retirement mainstay are requiring too much of their hard-earned retirement savings and equity from their current home sale. The lack of affordable homes is causing many Boomers to the jump into the rental market instead of investing in another house that is not in line with their fixed budget.

Nationwide Internet listing service, RENTCafé, helps renters locate apartment and rental homes throughout the US. RENTCafé released a report that proves it's the Baby Boomers, not Millennials, that are moving into the rental market. Since 2015, the percentage of the rental population over 55 years old jumped 28 percent. To compare, the increase in rental households for Millennials during the same period was just 3 percent. Boomer rental households jumped by nearly 2.5 million from 2009 to 2015, the largest increase by any generation. In the same time, Millennials saw an increase of just 500,000.

Many of the Baby Boomers who are opting to rent are choosing city life. While a larger percentage of Boomers choose to rent in the suburbs (39%), more than one in five choose to remain in urban areas. Baby Boomer's long-time family homes have appreciated dramatically over the past thirty years, so many of them are experiencing a real windfall when they sell. For those more affluent Boomers who choose to remain in the city, they are fueling the development of high-end urban independent living communities that provide everything they need; including access to high-quality healthcare, connection to public transportation, neighborhood walkability, and proximity to family.

One such upscale urban retirement community is Waterstone, located in Boston's exclusive Brighton neighborhood. With rents starting at $7,000 per month, Waterstone offers active urban-style living, without the hassle or overhead of ownership. But as developers begin building in anticipation of the wealthy members of the Silver Tsunami, another segment of the growing Boomer population will be low-income renters.

There are some seniors who have stayed in the same homes, built equity, and benefitted from retirement plans. Others have not been as fortunate. The lack of affordable homes and rental units is going to be a big challenge for retiring Boomers and the Millennials seeking to live on their own. Today, the US only serves about a third of the low-income, low-savings Boomers and Traditionalists who qualify for housing and rental assistance. If this rate does not improve by 2035, nearly 5 million eligible Baby Boomers will not receive housing aid. This will ultimately cause a senior housing divide in the US.

Many Boomers will be more cash-strapped in their retirement years than previous generations. A study from the George Washington University School of Business polled 5,000 pre-retiree Boomers between the ages of 51 and 61. The study found that 60 percent have at least one source of long-term debt, 30 percent had no retirement account, and 36 percent could not come up with $2,000 for an unexpected emergency. The Social Security Administration predicts that 41 percent of younger Boomers will lack sufficient income at age 67 to maintain pre-retirement income. That figure increases to 43 percent for Gen X. Because of this inevitable trend, developers need to be working closely with federal and local governments to build affordable senior housing.

Millennials are feeling the trickle-down effects of the Boomers' downsizing challenges. In addition to higher home prices, inventory is at an all-time low. The reduced inventory of affordable houses is forcing Baby Boomers to remain in their homes. Those homes stay out of the market and will not be available for young Millennial families to scoop up. Boomers that are downsizing are taking their equity and paying cash for over-inflated smaller homes that Millennials typically purchased as their first home. In most cases, Millennials can't pay cash and must finance their first homes. Banks and mortgage holders will only loan up to the appraised value. Boomers can pay more than appraised with their cash and that is a problem for Millennials who find themselves in bidding wars for properties.

More Boomers entering the rental market is also causing rents to rise across the US. Combine these trends with the fact that many Millennials face student debt, which significantly affects their debt-to-income ratios, and it is no surprise that many Millennials are living at home with their parents longer.

Despite the challenges, Millennials are positive about buying a home as an investment. In addition, Millennials have been the largest generation of home buyers for the past three years. Realtor.com reported that in 2016, 36 percent of mortgages went to buyers aged 25-34, increasing from 31 percent in 2015. They found that the reasons Millennials are buying homes included: an increase in income as they grow in their chosen careers, being tired of their current living arrangement, favorable interest rates, and increased rents.

The common Millennial stereotype is that they are all living in their parent's basement. Pew Research found that in 2017, 15 percent of Millennials were still living at home. With that said, they aren't being slackers. When interviewed, most said the primary reason they lived at home was to save money. They want to pay off their student loans and they want to save for a down payment. Sixty-four percent of Millennial first time home buyers bought a home for the pure desire of owning a place of their own.

As you can imagine, tech savvy Millennials are also radically changing the way homes are being researched, shown, and sold. Nearly two-thirds of adult Millennials start their real estate searches online through websites and mobile apps like Zillow, Trulia, and Realtor.com. Like so many sectors, this access to research is forcing realtors to become much more knowledgeable about relationship selling. Millennial buyers are calling them with a list of homes they want to see. By the time they get there, they already know the appraised value, market data, and historical information about the home.

Zillow, in particular, has been a major disruptor in the real estate industry. Zillow allows home sellers to list their own homes on the site, complete with pretty pictures and details that stand their own side-by-side with those listed by professional realtors. Zillow doesn't sell real estate, they sell ads to realtors. Since Millennials and most generations are so familiar with Zillow, realtors must advertise to have their listings compete in a crowded consumer-driven market.

If you are interested in learning more about how Zillow has changed the real estate landscape, I encourage you to read "Zillow Talk: The New Rules of Real Estate" by Zillow's CEO, and founding employee, Spencer Rascoff. Zillow is not only helping home buyers research the perfect home, they are collecting massive data from home sales all over the US. This data allows them to create "Zestimates," which estimates a home's value by assessing a host of data points around the home's address. One of the data points I found interesting is the "Starbucks Effect." Zillow can accurately predict that home prices and values will soar in areas where a Starbucks opens up. If you see a new Starbucks going up, that is where you want to buy.

Another real estate trend is the rise in multigenerational housing. Fifty-seven million people are living in a multigenerational household. The number has doubled since 1980. There are a few things driving this trend. Affordability is one factor, as I already mentioned many 20-somethings are choosing to live in their parent's household so that they can save.

Gen Xers and young Baby Boomers are finding themselves constantly switching between caring for their adult children and aging parents. One in five younger Boomers purchased a multigenerational home in the past five years. The costs for elder home care has escalated over the past decade, primarily due to the growing demand of an aging society. In most cases, it is less expensive to move your aging parents in with you, rather than spend upwards of $10,000 per month for senior care. Because of this dynamic, the demand for in-law suites has risen dramatically, with many opting for separate backyard living spaces instead of a pool.

If the young Millennials are not still living at home, chances are they are living in the city centers. Living in the city provides conveniences that Millennials seek. For instance, restaurants and health clubs are just a short walk away. Access to public transportation and an "Uber" at the touch of their smartphone allows them to live "car free." Maybe they don't even need a driver's license, as we noted in the iGen chapter. Things change once children come into the picture. Millennial parents will eventually gravitate to the suburbs, as a good school district often becomes priority over the commute time to work.

Finally, the GenXers wanted those McMansions with open floor plans, new kitchens with the stainless appliances, and an ensuite master bath. Millennials are seeking environmentally friendly homes with green heating and cooling, and energy-efficient appliances and lighting.

Chapter 13

Transportation

As you may expect, Millennials and their smartphones have been catalysts for change in the transportation industry. What you may not expect is that Baby Boomers have had an equally disrupting impact on car buying and ownership as well.

To better understand transportation trends, hop back to the real estate chapter. There is a direct correlation between where people choose to live and the modes of transportation required to meet their daily commuting needs. As you read in the previous chapters, both Boomers and Millennials are choosing to live in the city, more so than their parents and grandparents did at their age. Urbanization has a major impact on car buying and ownership.

When you live in an urban area, having an automobile can be a real hassle and very expensive. For example, if you choose to own a car in America's largest city, New York, the cost of parking alone can be more than the total cost to rent an apartment in the burbs. If you are in the market for a Big Apple apartment with a parking space, you can expect to shell out an additional $60,000 to upwards of $150,000 for that piece of asphalt. You can choose to use the city parking options at an average cost of $430 per month. The last option is to seek out street parking and then have to worry about alternating what side of the street to park on to accommodate street cleaning and trash collection. You would also have to deal with weather, especially in colder climates where it is not unusual to find your car buried in five feet of snow thanks to the snow plows.

These challenges are the norm in most of the country's larger cities. In addition to the costs associated with owning a car in the city, you must also deal with a lot of stress and anxiety.

As you learned in previous chapters, additional stress is not what younger generations seek or want. Driving in a big city's suffocating traffic and dodging millions of people on foot and on bikes, is stressful. Finding parking at your destination is also a challenge and can run you upwards of $50 for a few hours. Finding gas for your car is becoming more difficult in urban environments. Developers are keenly aware that an office, apartment building, and retail space fetches a much better return on investment than a single gas station. Fewer gas stations are available, and the cost of gas is higher than average. Finally, there is the stress of keeping your car in good shape. Scratches, dents, and the occasional ripped off mirror make it difficult and stressful to own and maintain a nice car in the city.

Urban areas also offer an abundance of transportation options. These include taxis, public transportation, and smartphone friendly rideshare options like Uber and Lyft. There are bikes and Zip Cars to be rented from one location and simply dropped off near your destination. Another trend in transportation is the popularity of peer-to-peer car sharing. Getaround is a company that makes it possible for someone to rent their car when he or she is not using it. This option makes it possible for cash-strapped Millennials and Boomers to earn extra income that could offset the expenses associated with car ownership. Getaround notes that the average car sits idle 86% of the time. The site mentions that it is possible to earn as much as $10,000 per year by sharing your car with others. This is music to the ears of debt-strapped Millennials and retired Baby Boomers who are living on a fixed income.

Millennials and Baby Boomers are choosing to live in urban areas for longer durations. For Millennials, being connected to the conveniences of the city is appealing. Around 2009, there was near panic in the auto industry as they wrestled with the thought of Millennials never buying a car. At the time, Millennials represented 30 percent of the population but only 17 percent of new car purchasers. Luckily, Baby Boomers were covering some of the slack and represented the largest generation of car buyers until 2015 when Millennials finally surpassed them. One of the reasons for the Millennial car buying boom was the fact that they started moving back to the suburbs as they grew older and started having children. As you learned in earlier chapters, Millennials are waiting longer to have children, so they also waited longer to move to the suburbs where they required an automobile for commuting.

As for Baby Boomers, they are also moving back to the cities in record numbers. They are opting for urban conveniences instead of the over-inflated costs of purchasing retirement homes in Florida or Arizona. When Boomers move back to the city, the need for an automobile decreases. Boomers are becoming more and more comfortable with technology and their smartphones; therefore, they are one of the fastest growing consumer segments for Uber and Lyft. They are also very open to driving for these companies since it affords them the opportunity to earn income. There is a social benefit as well, as retired Boomers can meet people and have interesting conversations with their riders. Ever notice how chatty Boomer Uber drivers are? Engage them if they engage you. It is amazing what you can learn from retiree Boomers. Most of them have had an interesting ride and they will be happy to share on your ride.

The types of cars Millennials are buying are much different from Boomers and Gen Xers. For Gen Xers and Boomers, the automobile was a rite of passage. It symbolized freedom. I remember having pictures of my dream cars on my bedroom wall when I was thirteen. I wanted that Black Trans Am with the Golden Eagle - the one Burt Reynolds drove in Smokey and the Bandit. I also dreamed about a 1965 Mustang convertible (and I still dream about that one today). I had friends that had them in high school and they were just "old hand-me-down cars." Find one today, and they cost ten to twenty times what they cost new. For older generations, their cars defined them, in a way. You could say a lot about a person's personality type based on the car they drove.

Millennials and iGens do not have the same relationships with cars as older generations. Remember, many Millennials and older iGens didn't even get their driver's licenses until they were in their twenties. When they did get a license, it was by necessity because mom or dad wasn't going to chauffeur them around anymore and their friend that had the car was gone, off to college. Millennials have grown up in the "sharing economy," so they are very comfortable calling an Uber, Lyft, or even using a peer-to-peer car sharing service. For younger Millennials, they tend to view transportation as an on-demand service, rather than having the fixed costs associated with car ownership.

Many Millennials are saddled with college debt, so they are not into sizeable car payments and other expenses associated with owning a new car. It may be difficult for them to get the credit needed to finance a car due to their low credit scores and out-of-whack debt to-income ratios. Therefore, younger generations are more pragmatic when shopping for an automobile. They look for value and rarely purchase more than they need. One of the top car choices for Millennials is the Toyota Prius, primarily due to its high gas mileage (around 50 mph).

There is one exception when Millennials will dig deeper into their wallets, and that is technology. They require their cars to have the latest tech and want them to seamlessly integrate with their smartphones.

Millennials are disrupting the way we buy cars today. According to a 2013 study by Dealer.com and GfK Automotive Research, 84 percent of car shoppers are on Facebook daily. Twenty-four percent of them used Facebook as a resource for making their vehicle purchases. There is a vast assortment of auto buying resource apps like Autotrader, Cars.com, and CarGurus where you can search for the perfect car by price, mileage, options, location, and even color. Those same apps can even tell you if the car has been wrecked and how it compares with similar cars for sale in the area.

Before a consumer steps foot in a showroom, it is safe to assume that they already know everything about the automobile they want. In many cases, consumers will visit a dealership only to test drive a car, and then go home to buy it online. If they ultimately purchase from a dealer, there is a growing number of consumers that prefer to start the buying process online, including credit checks and financing. They want to show up at the dealer, sign a few docs, get the keys and leave. No more haggling for hours and hours. Those days are gone.

While Millennials are driving the online research and purchasing trends, other generations are jumping on board. As a Gen X/Boomer Cusper, I very much felt like a

Millennial when we purchased our last car. We had a 2008 Volkswagen Touareg and absolutely loved the vehicle. It crossed 100 thousand miles, and we thought it might be time to consider a newer VW model. But wait, online reviews raved about the Subaru Outback, The Jeep Grand Cherokee, and the Volvo X90. Gen Xers are master online researchers. Sometimes, we research so much that we get paralyzed and confused. What we did know is that we wanted a newer used model with low miles. We never buy a new car.

We spent hours and hours researching all four models on the CarGuru app. Then we went to the dealerships to test drive each of the models. After all the test driving, we were even more convinced that we wanted another Touareg. So, then we set out to find the right one. We broadened our online search radius to 500 miles and found the perfect car at Donohoo Auto, just outside of Birmingham, Alabama, roughly 400 miles from home! Through the app, we contacted the dealer, and within an hour, we had the financing arranged, and a flight booked. A nice, young Millennial associate from Donohoo Auto picked us up at the airport in "our car," and we headed back to the dealership to buy the car. We were prepared for an all-day process, like the old days. To our surprise, we were in-and-out in about an hour.

I was so impressed with Donohoo Auto. They don't have a traditional showroom, but they do have over 700 used cars on their lot to choose from. When you walk in the front door, they have a few flat screen televisions with live sports and a line of six computer screens. You use the computer to select a car from their inventory. Within five minutes, the car is waiting for you in the front with the keys in it. You take the car for as long as you want, without a pushy salesperson in the back seat. You can really "test drive" the car the way you expect to drive it. In fact, you can test drive as many cars as you want.

Once you select the car you want, you start the process of financing, etc. There's no price haggling. The price is the price. There were a dozen or so helpful sales reps that do not get paid a commission. They are paid based on the overall success of the dealership, so everyone is eager to help.

Our experience was smooth, as we had already done the paperwork online prior to our arrival. Once we got there, we test drove the car for the first time, and it was everything we had hoped for. After we signed some papers, they gave us a Millennial "tech expert" who spent as much time as we needed explaining the massive amount of technology that our newer model VW featured. Technology in cars has come a long way since 2008. Wow!

I was so impressed with this new kind of car buying experience that I reached out to Chris Donohoo, a managing member of the Donohoo Auto family, to find out more about their story. I wanted to understand why my recent car buying experience was so different and so painless. They were on to something, and I was confident it had a lot to do with the Millennial's needs.

Chris told me that Donohoo Auto started precisely the opposite of most US auto dealers. Traditional auto dealers started with big lots and dozens of salespeople. They have had to move towards the online sales model and adapt to the new technologies that are disrupting the traditional car buying experience. Chris said, "Donohoo Auto started as a mom and pop dealership, selling on eBay and Yahoo

Auctions. We kept growing and adding folks. We haven't had to change that much, but we have adapted to a customer-centric philosophy that fits our outfit very well." As for Millennials, Donohoo was already operating in their sweet spot. "Millennials are used to quick, efficient "right now" transactions and Donohoo fits that mold well."

There is little doubt that technology has made it much easier to travel in and around cities. Technology has also disrupted the way we buy and drive cars. Although they came to the party a little later than past generations, Millennials have driven a lot of new trends in transportation and the way we move around. Once Millennials, and now iGens, get beyond their fear of driving and actually get a driver's license, they will continue driving technology in the transportation industry. And that is going to be fun to watch. We have already witnessed the advent of self-driving cars, and that is just the beginning.

Chapter 14

Pet Care

Millennials are the newest generation of pet owners and they are changing everything. Pets have been around for centuries and, for the most part, they've been a secondary component to the family unit. As you have learned in this book, Millennials are waiting longer to become homeowners, buy cars, and become parents. But one thing they are not postponing is pet ownership.

With older generations, it was customary to wait a while to get a pet. Your twenties and early thirties were focused on getting an education and starting a career. Having a pet was a burden to those aspirations. The pet came after you settled down and had a few kids. Then it was time to buy the family dog, cat, or hamster. Maybe you even started with a goldfish.

Millennials are not waiting to get on the pet bandwagon. The global research firm, Mintel, released a survey that found three-fourths of Americans in their 30s have dogs, and 51 percent have cats. That compares to just over 50 percent of the overall population with dogs, and 35 percent being cat owners. These findings come at a time when Millennials are half as likely to be married or living with a partner than they were fifty years ago. Millennial's demand for flexible work schedules and the fact that they are delaying parenthood and "adulting," has triggered an increase in pet ownership. In many ways, it's like pets are becoming a replacement for children. Some have even called dogs the "Millennial child." Pets are less expensive, require less responsibility, yet they can provide companionship for lonely Millennials.

Millennials have helped the pet industry grow 300 percent over the past decade to a record $63 billion in annual sales. Millennials aren't just buying pet food and taking their pets to the vet when there is something wrong. As you learned,

Millennials tend to be more savings savvy than previous generations; however, they are not frugal when it comes to their pets. Last year Americans spent a whopping $11 billion on pet-pampering products and services alone. Mintel found that one-third of pet owners said they bought toys for their pets, while 17 percent purchased pet costumes. Ten percent even purchased a pet stroller for Fido.

Another survey from Wakefield Research found that 76 percent of Millennials admit that they are more likely to splurge on their pets than on themselves. They are more likely to spend their hard-earned money on expensive gourmet treats (44 percent), or a custom pet bed (38 percent). By comparison, less than 50 percent of Baby Boomers said they would splurge on their pets.

I have been a loyal "dog person" for most of my life. My wife introduced me to her Persian cat when we met, and for a while, I will admit I was also a "cat person." My iGen/Millennial cusper son is also an avid pet lover. So much so, he works with pets at Petco, where he has been employed for the past three years. Petco and PetSmart are the two largest pet retailers. Between them, they own and operate more than 3,000 retail locations throughout North America. Petco, PetSmart, and other pet retailers have experienced tremendous growth over the past decade (and you can thank Millennials for a lot of that growth).

I reached out to Brock Weatherup, a good friend from one of my past corporate gigs. Brock was CEO and co-founder of PetCoach. PetCoach focused on revolutionizing how "Pet Parents" engage with veterinarians to improve the health and lives of their pets. PetCoach provides pet owners free advice from highly skilled and verified veterinarians through their website and smartphone app. The app also keeps track of their pet's health at all times and connects with their veterinarian from the comfort of their home.

PetCoach speaks directly to Millennials by helping them manage their pet's health from their smartphones. As you can imagine, PetCoach is very well received by Millennials and other "Pet Parents." So much so that PetCoach was acquired by Petco in March 2017 and is now offered through Petco's expanding digital offerings. Brock is currently the Executive Vice President of Strategic Innovation and Digital Experience at Petco.

I asked Brock to give me some insight into how Millennials have changed the pet industry. He reiterated what I had previously discussed by confirming that pets are replacing children for the twenty-somethings. "Millennials are delaying having kids and they are using pets as an intro to child rearing," Brock said. "Younger Millennials seem to be using pets to manage their loneliness. They are completely redefining how pets fit into the family."

If you remember the iGen chapter, we discussed the mental health crisis with today's teens. Many young Millennials in their twenties suffer from anxiety and depression - and those conditions can often lead to loneliness. If you are a pet owner, you understand how pets can be healers in many ways. They can fill a void, and this could be what we are seeing with young Millennials.

Because pets have become "starter children" for young Americans today, they are elevating their pets to the same level that many place their children. Like most parents, Millennials want nothing but the best for their "practice kids." Today's pets are treated like family. They give their pets the highest quality, most nutritious food, and splurge on non-essential items while sacrificing similar purchases for themselves, as we mentioned earlier.

Brock has seen this trend develop over the past decade. "Pets are now more than just pets. They are equals in the family dynamic. Thirty years ago, if your dog was diagnosed with cancer, you didn't hesitate to put him down. Today, it is a much bigger decision that is not taken as lightly as in the past." Evidence of this trend is the rapid growth of specialty and emergency pet hospitals that treat everything from pet allergies, to cancer and rare diseases.

Blue Pearl Veterinary Partners is one example of a successful, emerging specialty pet hospital chain. Blue Pearl is a national provider of specialty and emergency veterinary care centers that have expanded across the US. Their website says, "We have hospitals located throughout the country, most are open 24 hours a day, every day of the year. Our veterinarians use innovative procedures, high-tech equipment, and the latest treatment methods to provide comprehensive medical care for your pets. We combine this expertise with a love for animals and the belief that kindness is the foundation of veterinary medicine."

When pet owners finally accept that their best friend has a chronic, life-threatening condition, they often spend thousands of dollars doing everything they can do to make their pet's last days on earth the best they can be. It is not uncommon to find stories about people adjusting their lifestyle to accommodate a sick and dying pet. One of those stores is from Lauren Fern Watt.

When Lauren found out her beloved English Mastiff had only a few months to live, she created a bucket list for her best friend. They went canoeing, visited Time Square, ate lobster in Maine, and she became even closer to her best friend while sharing new experiences together. You may have seen the television ad created by Subaru called "Dream Weekend." The 60-second storyline follows a man and his fourteen-year-old dog on one last weekend road trip together in their Subaru. Subaru regularly targets Millennials in their advertising; however, if you have ever had to put your best friend to sleep, you can relate - no matter what generation you are.

Brock went on to talk about how Millennials are changing the way pet food is created and marketed as well. "Millennials changed the food industry when they started reading food labels. They started to question ingredients and began to demand sustainable, organic and healthier options. They have changed the food and restaurant industry. Now they are looking at pet food labels and demanding the same nutritious options for their pets."

Gen Xers remember being able to buy a fifty-pound bag of Purina Dog Chow or a bag of Meow Mix for around $10. This would feed their dog or cat for an entire month. Every Gen Xer remembers that catchy Meow Mix commercial... Sing along now...."Meow, meow, meow, meow... Meow, meow, meow, meow ...Meow, meow, meow, meow, meow, meow, meow, meow..."

Today, Millennial pet owners can spend upwards of $10 per day on their pet's meals. Look around Petco or your local pet store, and you see bags of pet food featuring vegetables, ducks, venison, salmon, and images of your dog being "the wolf that he is." Nutritious pet food options go beyond traditional pet supply chains as well. The Millennial-driven nutritional, organic pet food trend has given rise to dog food companies like California-based "Just Food for Dogs."

Just Food for Dogs delivers hand-crafted meals for your pet, directly to your doorstep. It's like NutriSystem for dogs. They even have ten retail locations in Southern California where they prepare the meals in "kitchens." One quick visit to their website and you see that they are targeting Millennial "Pet Parents."

"Think Outside the Bag. Freshly prepared meals made from human-grade ingredients that are approved by the USDA. It is food for dogs... not dog food!" They use those tried and true Millennial marketing buzzwords as well. "Open. Honest. Just come tour the only open kitchens in the pet food business and watch your dog's food being made."

Now that you know Millennial pets are better fed, you probably noticed that they are showing up all over your social media feeds. Every generation has snapped photos of their children and shared them in family albums. Now social media has taken that custom to the next level. Since pets are the Millennial's "starter kids," they are seizing every opportunity to photograph and videotape their pets doing all kinds of cute and wacky stuff.

As you have learned in this book, and most likely seen for yourself, Millennials and iGens are online exhibitionists. Ninety-five percent of Millennials are on social media networks, and they are using them to share pictures of their four-legged best friend. It seems everyone loves cute pet pics and vids. Millennial "dog parents" watch dog videos or look at other dog photos on social media three times per week, on average. Eleven percent of Millennials, an estimated 3.5 million, have even created a separate social media profile for their dog.

There are a host of pet celebrities on Instagram, Facebook, and YouTube. Since I am a proud pug owner, I am a big fan of @itsdougthepug on Instagram. Doug is a three-year-old Pug with a whopping 9 million social media followers, and over a billion video views. His Millennial owner, Leslie Mosier, quit her job in the Nashville music industry to manage her dog full time. Doug the Pug has been photographed with Ed Sheeran, kissed by Justin Bieber and he re-created a Katy Perry music video while wearing a blue wig.

Petco recognized this trend and launched the app "Heads & Tails." They bill it as "the first iOS app where you can win money for taking cute pet selfies." Brock was amazed that the app registered over 300 thousand likes in its first ten days.

As a parent, you would never leave your three-year-old at home alone. Millennials are not leaving their dogs at home either. Restaurants and retailers are taking note and are going out of their way to make their establishments pet friendly. Many restaurants provide water bowls and some even have dedicated pet menus to entice Millennials to dine with their pets.

Millennial pet owners are socially conscious. Petco often sponsors local pet adoption events and always has cats available for adoption in their stores. Brock told me that the Millennials have changed the way pets are acquired as well.

They are much more in tune with the nation's challenge with homeless pets and have no mercy for shelters that euthanize those pets who don't get adopted in a reasonable time. This explains the rise in no-kill shelters across the country. Brock said, "30 years ago, 75 percent of dogs were purchased from breeders or pet stores. Today, it is less than 50 percent because Millennials would rather help society by adopting a pet."

Finally, I asked Brock what kinds of dogs Millennials prefer. For the past thirty years the top three dog breeds have been consistent: the Labrador, German Shepherd, and the Golden Retriever. Millennials tend to favor the designer breeds like Labradoodles and Puggles. They like to be different and stand out. Baby Boomers would have never thought there would be a day when you could order a hypoallergenic dog.

Chapter 15

Volunteering & Philanthropy

Volunteerism is a passion of mine. As you learned in the introduction, I spent two decades managing cause marketing programs in schools with the support of fortune 500 companies. Nearly all of the programs required parent and community volunteer support. In my latter years in corporate America, I spent a few years engaging more than a million Millennial parent volunteers for a children's book publisher that hosted literacy events in schools. Without the support of parent volunteers, many school fundraising programs could not exist.

In my personal life, my family and I frequently donate to worthy causes and try to volunteer whenever we can. We are constantly looking for ways to help people in our community and throughout the Caribbean who need it most. What is cool and relevant is that we volunteer as a family. Our iGen/Millennial cusper son loves to go on mission trips with his GenX/Boomer cusper parents, and that is a trend that is growing.

I have great admiration for those who donate their hard-earned money or volunteer their time for the benefit of others. One organization that has a long history of helping communities through volunteerism is Kiwanis. Kiwanis is a 100-year-old international organization that has one simple goal - to help make the world a better place, one child at a time. There are other international service organizations that do great work as well like Rotary International, the Lions Club, Elks, Eagles, and many more.

As a Kiwanis member, I often speak at Kiwanis conferences across the US on the topic of intergenerational engagement. Kiwanis, as well as many service organizations, is experiencing an age-diversity challenge. Sixty-three percent of Kiwanis members are Boomers or older. Boomer and Traditionalists are finding that they have more time to volunteer, especially after they retire. Many join service organizations like Kiwanis, which is full of like-minded people who are united for the common cause of serving the community. I have never met a more passionate, caring group of people than the older Kiwanians. I am especially impressed with their passion for helping children. Kiwanis and most other century-old service organizations are all in the same boat. How do they change and adapt to meet the needs of busy Gen Xers and Millennials without losing the heritage that their older members worked so hard to build?

One of the ways Kiwanis is addressing the challenge is by leveraging their Service Learning Programs (SLPs). Many people don't know that Key Club is Kiwanis. Key Club is a teen student-led service group that is present in nearly every high school. Key Club is experiencing a rapid growth, while the Adult Kiwanis Clubs are struggling to build membership. Kiwanis also has Circle K on college campuses in addition to Builder's Club and K Kids for middle and elementary schools.

Key Club and Circle K are growing because of the iGens and their love of service. You read about their passion for social impact and making the world a better place in the iGen chapter. Millennials and iGens were the first generations required to perform community service to graduate from high school. They have been trained to volunteer, and that is following them into adulthood. That is a very good thing. The younger generation's passion for community service and social impact is helping the Kiwanis SLPs grow. So, where do they go after college? Why don't they jump

219

immediately into an adult Kiwanis Club? The main reasons are careers and kids. They simply get too busy.

Based on what you have read so far, one would think that volunteerism in America is on the rise. Younger generations are more socially conscious than any prior generation. With 10,000 Baby Boomers retiring every day, you would think there would be an onslaught of bored new retirees looking for something to do. Despite those trends, volunteerism in America is down.

Since 2002, the Bureau of Labor Statistics has issued a report on volunteer rates in the United States. The volunteer rate has been steadily declining over the past five years. In 2015, the U.S. volunteer rate was 24.9 percent. About 62.6 million people volunteered through, or for, an organization at least once in 2015.

Volunteering by generation and age varies. Gen Xers were the most likely to volunteer at 28.9 percent. Volunteer rates were lowest among the youngest Millennials at 18.4 percent; however, they volunteer more once they graduate from college and start their careers. iGen teenagers, like the Key Clubbers, continued to have a relatively high volunteer rate, at 26.4 percent. Over the years, the volunteer rates for younger Gen Xers, aged 35-to-44, and younger Baby Boomers, aged 55-to-64, has declined. No one knows why, but it could be that the younger Gen Xers are entering a pretty tough time in child rearing. All those birthday parties and practices get in the way of volunteering. The younger Boomers may be putting their heads down for one more big career push so that they can bank the most income for their upcoming retirement, but those are just assumptions.

Volunteer organizations are quickly learning that technology is key if they want to engage younger volunteers. Schools, who historically have a tough time recruiting and engaging parent volunteers, are finding greater success of late by using online and app-based services like VolunteerSpot, SignUpGenius and others. These services allow volunteer coordinators to manage all their activities, scheduling, and volunteer communications in one place. Volunteers receive notifications through their smartphones.

One of the pioneers in technology-enabled volunteer recruitment is VolunteerMatch. VolunteerMatch is a nonprofit organization that believes everyone should have the chance to make a difference. They were truly ahead of their time. Prior to VolunteerMatch, nonprofit organizations and charities found it difficult to recruit volunteers for their events and projects. They had to rely on outbound calling and word-of-mouth. If you were someone who was looking for a volunteer opportunity, there was no central source to easily identify where you may be needed. VolunteerMatch was founded in 1998. Today they are the largest volunteer engagement network, serving 100,000 participating nonprofits and more than 13 million annual visitors by matching them with volunteer opportunities through their website. Since its launch, VolunteerMatch has helped the social sector attract more than $6.8 billion worth of volunteer services.

Scott Lohman is VolunteerMatch's Senior Vice President and he manages their business solutions team. His team works with corporations to build internal volunteer platforms for their employees. In a recent interview with Scott, he told me that business was booming, thanks to the Millennials who are demanding that their employers offer company-sponsored volunteer opportunities. Companies are aware of this need and know they must actively and publicly promote their social impact to recruit, engage, and retain their growing Millennial workforce. To help them simplify the process, they are using the VolunteerMatch technology internally to match their employee's social and societal passions with local or virtual opportunities that allow them to serve others.

I asked Scott to give me some examples of how generational changes have altered his business and volunteering over the past decades.

As mentioned above, younger Millennials, in particular, are all about "passion before paycheck." Don't get me wrong, salary and compensation are still important to Millennials, but corporate culture and a host of other issues, like professional growth, are equally as important. Many of those were discussed in the Millennial chapter. As you read, 60 percent of Millennials have indicated that they will not be at their current job in three years. That puts a lot of stress on human resource departments. They consistently wrestle with decisions regarding how much to invest on new Millennial employees, only to see them leave.

There is one thing that nearly all Millennials agree on when it comes to where they decide to work. They want their company to stand for more than just the bottom line. They want their job to matter and have a greater purpose. One of the ways to meet that need is for companies to encourage community service and volunteerism. This should be encouraged from the CEO down, and should be woven into the company culture.

"In the San Francisco Bay area, tech companies who employ a lot of younger Millennial coders and programmers are finding it very hard to compete for talent." Scott said. "Some of the things we are seeing is tech companies creating CSR (corporate social responsibility) teams and encouraging their Millennial employees to join the teams and contribute."

Most of the large fortune 100 companies have foundations and separate divisions dedicated to social impact. In many ways, they are set, according to Scott. "VolunteerMatch is seeing tremendous growth in small and mid-sized companies who are requesting their services - evidence that it's helping them compete for Millennials." It's not just volunteer time, they are also making a difference with their wallets. Scott also told me that Millennials are making regular donations. "On average, Millennials are donating 10 percent of their income to charities."

VolunteerMatch has connected over 13 million volunteers with nonprofit opportunities. Like Zillow, they have been able to collect a massive amount of data on volunteer behaviors and trends. They can see what types of causes are getting the most support and the ones that are losing support. I was curious to know what the top causes were for Millennial volunteers.

According to Scott, Millennials prefer volunteer opportunities that benefit their local community. They also seek volunteer opportunities around advocacy and social justice like inclusion, diversity, and women's rights. Environmental causes also rank very high for Millennials.

One of the negative trends Scott has seen over the past five years is a decline in volunteers seeking to help religious

223

organizations. This makes sense because younger Millennials have been turning away from the church, and religion in general. Once they have kids, they start to go back. Scott also thinks the falling trend could be attributed to the Traditionalists and older Boomers passing on or getting to a point where they can no longer physically volunteer. This also makes sense because older Americans are historically more religious.

One of the most interesting observations Scott shared with me was the impact the 2016 presidential election had on Millennials. The day after the Presidential Inauguration was the largest day in the history of VolunteerMatch. 80,000 people visited VolunteerMatch on that day (which was three times their daily average). Most of them were looking for volunteer opportunities that pertained to human rights and women's rights, two heavily publicized issues that President Trump faced during the election. Younger Millennials tend to vote Democrat, so they wasted no time looking for ways to make an impact. As you learned before, Millennials simply do not "accept." Unlike the Silent's before them, they do not hesitate to challenge the status quo.

Millennials are also responsible for a rise in "skills-based volunteering." Scott says, "They really don't get excited about painting a fence or delivering Meals on Wheels like older generations. They would rather use their career skills to help a cause. It's a bonus if they can volunteer virtually." Scott goes on to say, "They are even looking for multinational volunteer opportunities, but not like the old days when you joined the Peace Corps. They may want to use their skills to help a nonprofit in Uganda build an excel spreadsheet to manage their finances, and they can do that from their bedroom in the US."

Another trend in volunteerism is the inclusion of "giving platforms." The younger, more tech-savvy philanthropists want the ability to make a donation in lieu of, or in addition to, volunteering. VolunteerMatch does not offer that service and companies are now demanding that feature. Collecting cash and credit card payments is a challenge, but there are organizations that specialize in that. Those companies don't offer Volunteer Matching and, even if they did, they can't offer over a million opportunities like VolunteerMatch. To address the challenge, VolunteerMatch has been partnering with online giving platforms, like BrightFunds and YourCause, that now offer Millennials the opportunity to find volunteer opportunities and donate to them through one link on their company portal. This combination of giving time and money hits the Millennial sweet spot. If your company is not offering this as an employee benefit, you are missing the boat and you may be missing your Millennial employees in three years.

Like every other industry, mass adoption of smartphones has played a big role in volunteer engagement. Five years ago, only 25 percent of VolunteerMatch users accessed the site through their mobile device. Today nearly 60 percent of all interaction occurs via mobile. Volunteer coordinators can be on the beach for a "beach cleanup" project and check in volunteers on their smartphone.

Donations by smartphone is preferred by Millennials and even Gen Xers. Giving them the ability to Tweet a hashtag or send a text to donate has been very successful. In the 2017 World Series, T-Mobile donated $20,000 for every home run hit in the series. In addition, they donated $2 for every tweet or retweet of the hashtag #HR4HR. There were over 600,000 tweets and a record 21 home runs. When the last out was recorded in game seven and the Houston Astros were celebrating their first World Series Win, T-Mobile was writing a check for over $2.5 million to support hurricane relief efforts in Houston. I am willing to bet that the majority of those 600,000 tweets came from Millennial smartphones. This is a prime example of the power of coupling donors with technology.

Summary

As I finish writing this book amid the hectic holiday season, I look around me and I see many opportunities to engage with and learn from a hundred years' worth of experience and knowledge.

The holidays are about family and reflection. I see television commercial after television commercial showing large families "getting along." iGen children are opening presents under the tree, with proud parents and grandparents watching from the couch while admiring their multigenerational offspring. A chiseled, square-jawed, Millennial man, is giving a nice diamond necklace to his beautiful girlfriend as she gives him "that look." A Gen Xer, accompanied by their kids in pajamas who are frantically running around the Christmas tree, looks out his or her window on a snowy Christmas morning to find a shiny new Mercedes, wrapped in a big red bow, in the driveway. I always wondered why there was no snow on the car. And, who does that anyway?

In between the holiday commercials that are showcasing the perfect harmony of the large, extended, multigenerational family, there are the classic holiday movies, featuring dysfunctional families - which, in my opinion, are a little more realistic.

We love to watch little Ralphie's imagination run wild as he fantasizes about saving his family and the world with his new Red Ryder BB Gun. Those dreams are dashed as his mom, dad, teacher, and even Santa tell him, "You'll shoot your eye out!" In the 1940's, children, like Ralphie, were free to let their mind wander, imagine, and create. What if little Ralphie had a smartphone? Would he have had the mental capacity to "dream" about all of the great accomplishments that the Red Ryder BB Gun could bring? Or, would he have stayed in his room, head down, tuned out, anxious and depressed from seeing all of his friends get their Red Ryder BB Guns on social media?

The all-time best dysfunctional holiday family is featured in the movie "Christmas Vacation." The Griswold kids are stressed and unhappy, the crazy uncle arrives uninvited, with no money or gifts for his family. Mom does everything she can to keep the peace and, of course, Clark Griswold dreams of the perfect holiday and then goes way out of his way to create his version, for the entire multigenerational family. That movie is a great example of the communication challenges between generations within the family. But, in the end, it all works out.

Families are together from birth, and they have a lot of time through the years to learn about each other, find common ground, and eventually help each other when necessary. After all, it's family. Businesses can have the same generational dynamics at play. Your work family is not much different from your extended family. You must work harder to bridge the generations at the office because you don't have the years of history and personal knowledge about your coworkers. That can be a good thing, because you don't have preconceived notions or history to shape your opinions.

When it comes to generations in the workplace, in schools, or in your own household, you have a unique opportunity to learn from, and share your story with others. We all have generational sign posts that shaped us into who we are today. Those sign posts became the foundations for our own stories. To achieve intergenerational harmony, you must first become self-aware and understand why you may feel a certain way. Then, you must understand the other generational personalities and their values, and not judge them based on your experiences alone. When you understand all five generations, you will become your own "Intergenerational Engagement Expert." You will be able to embrace your co-worker's experiential strengths instead of dismissing them and labeling them as "out of touch."

I hope this book delivered enough general information to help you become self-aware of your own generation as well as other generation's values and preferences. If you have been confused, you may have learned that you are a Cusper, and you are normal. Now you have the opportunity to look at your extended family, your work family, or your school family and ask yourself: Do I want my center of influence to be like the perfect family holiday commercial or do I want it to be more like Clark Griswold's family? More than likely, this information has given you the knowledge to land somewhere in the middle. That's real life. Good luck.

Here are some cheat sheets to help you remember the key characteristics of each generation:

You can download copies of these sheets for free at www.5-gens.com

The Silent Generation - Traditionalists

Generational Stats	Sign Posts that Shaped Their Generation	Values and Characteristics	Work and Career
• Born between 1928 - 1945 • U.S. population -28.3 million • Representing 2% of the U.S. labor force at 3.7 million	• The Great Depression • World War II • The Cold War • McCarthyism • The beginnings of the Civil Rights Movement • As children, they were "Seen but not Heard."	• Hardworking • Preferred communications method is the written word • Dedication to the USA - Patriotic • Loyal • "Waste not want not" mentality • Expect respect of their seniority • Stayed at one company for life with pension, and retirement • Demand quality	• Prefer one-on-one communication and in-person meetings • Need explicit instructions • Expects feedback only when something needs correcting; No news is good news • Possess great interpersonal skills • Team players • Measure work ethic on timeliness, productivity, and not drawing attention

The Baby Boomers

Generational Stats	Sign Posts that Shaped Their Generation	Values and Characteristics	Work and Career
• Born between 1946 - 1964 • U.S. population -75.5 million • Representing 29% of the U.S. labor force at 44.6 million	• Assassinations of JFK, Robert Kennedy, Martin Luther King, Jr. • The Space Race and Walk on the Moon • Vietnam War • Protests and sit-ins • Woodstock • Civil rights, Women's rights, and environmental Movements • Watergate- Nixon Resignation • Self-discovery	• Preferred communications method is a phone call • Work/career centric • Family • Morality • Workaholics / expects everyone to go the extra mile • Buys to impress others • Demands quality products and services • Very loyal to brands • Wants respect from younger generations	• Seeks professional development • Expects raises and career advancement • Expects leadership role • Power, title, praise, and public recognition • Enjoys in-person meetings • Introduced a less formal style - using first names at work • Prefers all team members work from same office

231

Generation X - The Forgotten Generation

Generational Stats	Sign Posts that Shaped Their Generation	Values and Characteristics	Work and Career
• Born between 1965 - 1980 • U.S. population -65.7 million • Representing 33% of the U.S. labor force at 52.7 million	• End of the Vietnam War and Cold War • Fall of the Berlin Wall • AIDS • MTV • Microwave Dinners • Computers - AOL • Grunge, Hip-Hop, and Rap Music • Challenge Explosion • Reganomics	• Latchkey kids • Independent and Creative • Preferred communications method is e-mail, text second • Focused on results, not policies • Needs to be engaged, have fun • Demands many options • Wants cost savings • Responds to relationship-focussed selling	• Demands work-life-balance • Comfortable working virtually • Informal, uses humor often • Self-starters • Largely about relationship building • Little patience for "paying your dues" • Needs to be creative with solutions • Doesn't respond well to micro-management

Generation Y - The Millennials

Generational Stats	Sign Posts that Shaped Their Generation	Values and Characteristics	Work and Career
• Born between 1981 - 1998 • U.S. population -79.4 million • Representing 34% of the U.S. labor force at 53.5 million	• Rise of the Internet • First Laptop • CDs and DVDs • Columbine Shooting • Waco Massacre • Y2K • September 11th • Terrorism and the War on Terror • OJ Simpson Trial • Exxon Valdez Oil Spill • The Introduction of Social Media • Invasion of Iraq	• Over-parented - Helicopter parents • Texting is how they communicate, use their smartphones for everything except talking • Expects companies to be transparent, socially conscious and use sustainable practices • Feel they can do or be anything they want • Diversity is the norm • Believe they can change the world	• Value lifestyle vs. climbing the company ladder • Results oriented vs time clock • Require constant feedback and evaluation • Innovators, risk-takers, not afraid off making mistakes • Entrepreneurial • Craves meaningful work • Not loyal, will leave if not happy • Corporate Social Responsibility is key

232

iGen - Generation Z

Generational Stats	Sign Posts that Shaped Their Generation	Values and Characteristics	Work and Career What to Know on Day
• Born after 1999 • U.S. population -73.6 million • Representing 2% of the U.S. labor force at 3.2 million	• The Great Recession • Digital Natives: Do not remember a time without Smartphones and the Internet • Social Media • Mental Illness Epidemic- Anxiety and Depression • Obama Presidential term • 2016 election and Donald Trump as a celebrity and The President • Opioid Epidemic	• Digital Natives - The World at their fingertips • Always ON - 8 sec attention span • Social Responsible • Delaying "adulting" • More like the Silent Generation, their Great Grandparents • Active in social media but not sharing as much as Millennials • Family relationships important • Shops brick & mortar	• Willing to work harder than previous generations for advancement • Desire long-term learning and development from day one • Want job-security, good benefits and a retirement program • They don't want a boss, they want a mentor/coach • Many come to the workplace with a lot of internship experience

 **D. KNIGHT** Marketing & Consulting Group   www.dknightmarketing.com

Acknowledgements

Through my career and journey through life, I have had many mentors, coaches, good bosses, and challenging bosses. I would like to acknowledge those who provided interviews and counseled me on the writing of this book. Many are leading experts in their field and have written books and articles on their subjects of expertise. I have provided links to those books and I highly encourage you to read them for a deeper understanding of their areas.

Linda (Boomer/GenX Cusper Wife & Best Friend), **Jordan** (Millennial/iGen Cusper Son), **Kirsten** (Gen X Sister), **Penelope** (Silent/Baby Boomer Cusper Mom), and **Joe** (Silent/Baby Boomer Cusper Father, God rest your soul).

Your five generational insights and encouragement throughout my life cannot be underestimated. You have each inspired, and still inspire me every day. I love you all.

Deborah Gilboa, MD, aka "Dr. G." Parenting Expert and Keynote Speaker. Author of many books including, "Get the Behavior You Want… Without Being the Parent You Hate!"

I met Deborah years ago when we shared the stage at a social media influencers conference. Deborah has been a great resource and mentor ever since.

Yosi Heber: Founder and President, Oxford Hill Partners, LLC

Yosi was the Chief Marketing Officer when I was at Entertainment Publications, Inc. Interestingly enough, many of my expert contributors spent some time at EPI. I am in awe of the levels of success those early EPI folks achieved. Yosi was always a big supporter of my creative programs while at EPI and was a valued friend and mentor when I re-launched my marketing and consulting business in 2016.

Carl Venters: Independent Broadcast Media Professional. Past Chairman, Voyager Communications. Past President, North Carolina Association of Broadcasters. Past Vice Chairman of The National Association of Broadcasters.

Carl was a good friend of my father and owned radio stations when I was growing up in Raleigh, North Carolina. Carl recognized my love for radio and mentored me through my career in broadcasting. Since my father's passing in 2012, Carl stepped in and he gladly offers me his fatherly advice to this day.

Maria Bailey: Mom Engagement Expert, Foremost Global Marketing to Moms Expert, Author, Host of Mom Talk Radio, and CEO at BSM Media, Inc.

I have followed Maria's expert advice on family marketing strategies for more than a decade. "Advertising Age" magazine credits her for coining the phrase, "Marketing to Moms." Maria's company, BSM Media helps organizations like HP, Huggies, Beaches Resorts, and more reach moms.

Chris Soechtig: Former Senior Vice President of Sales and Operations at iHeartMedia and current Market President at iHeartMedia, Tampa-St. Pete.

Chris and I have worked together for more than a decade on revenue-producing media campaigns that provide positive social impact in local communities. He has been an invaluable asset for all things media. Chris is also the most incredible fisherman I know.

Gayle Troberman: Chief Marketing Officer at iHeartMedia.

Gayle leads all marketing for iHeartMedia, formally Clear Channel Radio. iHeartMedia owns and operates 858 broadcast radio stations, serving more than 150 markets throughout the US. They also own the popular iHeartRadio app. Their top-rated music app streams radio stations from coast to coast and spans every popular genre and era - including pop, country, urban, rock, talk, and comedy. The iHeartRadio app has more than 100 million registered users.

Scott Lohman: VP, Sales and Marketing at VolunteerMatch.

Scott and I first worked together twenty years ago at Entertainment Publications. He spent some time at Groupon and other Bay area tech companies before landing at VolunteerMatch. Scott is passionate about social impact and has helped VolunteerMatch align with companies that want to leverage VolunteerMatch's vast network of nonprofit organizations and their volunteer opportunities. Since Millennials are demanding companies to be more socially conscious, Scott's efforts are burgeoning at a perfect time. His insights on how different generations look at volunteering and philanthropy were very helpful.

Mike Scott: Former Regional President, Mid-South, iHeartMedia.

Mike is one of the most creative media people I know. He has never encountered a project that he cannot take to the next level. While at Clear Channel Radio in New Orleans, Mike and I generated a lot of new station revenues while connecting tens of thousands of underserved kids with books to support their independent reading. We continued the momentum when he moved to West Palm Beach. Mike and I have become great friends, and he is still my first "go-to" person when it comes to creating media-driven social impact strategies.

Brock Weatherup: EVP Strategic Innovation and Digital Experience, PETCO.

Brock also worked with me at Entertainment Publications where he was one of the first digital marketers at the company. After leaving EPI, Brock became CEO of Fathead and has since founded two successful online pet companies. His first company, Pet360, was acquired by Petsmart, and the second, PetCoach, was recently acquired by PETCO, where he remains today. Brock was instrumental in providing me information on generational changes in the pet industry.

Dr. Jean M. Twenge: Professor of Psychology at San Diego State University.

Jean Twenge is the author of more than 130 scientific publications and six books, including the book I referred to in the iGen chapter, "iGen: Why Today's Super-Connected Kids Are Growing Up Less Rebellious, More Tolerant, Less Happy–and Completely Unprepared for Adulthood."

I have been following Dr. Twenge's writing for a while now, starting with her book "Generation Me," about Millennials. Dr. Twenge takes her research to another level. When looking at generational analysis, many base observations from just one survey. Dr. Twenge uses long-range surveys that have been active for decades across several generations.

She also uses focus groups to learn even more. Her latest book convinced me to use the term iGen to describe teens today.

Tom Kersting: Renowned Psychotherapist, long-time high school counselor, and author of the book "Disconnected: How to Reconnect Our Digitally Distracted Kids."

Tom provided me insights on how screen time is affecting teens.

Chris Donohoo: Dealer Principal at Donohoo Chevrolet LLC and Donohoo Auto LLC.

I met Chris when I traveled 300 miles to purchase an automobile from his company, Donohoo Auto. I was so impressed with their digital sales and marketing process that I interviewed Chris to find out whether generational preferences were responsible for their way of doing business. If you are in the market for a nice used car and want a turn-key shopping and purchasing experience, I highly recommend considering Donohoo Auto, just outside of Birmingham, Alabama. www.donohooauto.com

Jack Levine: Founder 4Generationas Institute.

Jack and I are fellow members of Kiwanis International. Jack speaks about the generations and breaks them into four segments: Younger than 25, 25-to-50, 50-to-75, and over 75. Jack lives in Tallahassee, Florida's capital and governmental hot spot. He is close to Florida State University, where he has a wealth of multi-generational subjects. Jack specializes in community activism and engagement within generations. He encourages bringing generations together to learn from each other. His insights on the differences between the "4Gens" were fascinating and helpful.

Bill Barrett, Anne Lee, Ann Amstutz-Hayes, and Evan St. Lifer: Senior Executives at Scholastic

I had the pleasure of working with Bill, Anne, Ann, and Evan during my ten years at Scholastic. They supported me and embraced my creativity in developing new programs that helped connect underserved kids with books to promote independent reading. iGens are not reading, and that is a big problem. Many at Scholastic, and other wonderful literacy organizations, are trying their best to fix it against all odds, "the smartphone."

Todd Smith, Florida Governor Kiwanis International, **Pam Norman, and Elizabeth Warren** with Kiwanis International.

As fellow Kiwanians, you inspire me to continue working with Kiwanis and the Kiwanis youth service leadership organizations to make the world a better place, one child at a time. I enjoy every opportunity you give me to speak about the generations with Kiwanians around the world.

Cynthia Blackwell & Wendy Sellers: Founders and Managing Partners of Blackrain Partners.

Cynthia and Wendy run an outstanding company that provides all levels of business coaching. They brought me into their organization to help coach their clients on Intergenerational Engagement, Personalities, and Sales Training. I enjoy any opportunity to speak, coach, and help companies and their people. They gave me more opportunities to do that.

Sean Donovan: Health Advocate and Authorpreneur, Author of "The BookBook: a Recipe for Writing and Publishing Your Book."

Sean is my friend and the editor of this book. We met shortly after moving to Ormond Beach, Florida at a Chamber of Commerce networking group. I told Sean I was interested in writing a book. He opened the trunk of his Mustang and handed me a copy of his book, "The BookBook." I read it on a short flight to New York City the next day. It was his book that inspired me to 'START!' I highly encourage anyone who has ever dreamed of writing a book, to seek out Sean's book and his services.

I have always been a master networker and have had the pleasure of having thousands of friends, and experts to go to when I needed advice, mentoring, and consultation. There are way too many others to thank or mention in this acknowledgment. If you are out there, reading this book, you know who you are. I would like to say, "Thank You." I hope that I have been a great mentor, friend and expert consultant for just as many.

Recommended Books and Resources:

Parenting:
www.askdoctorg.com
Check out Dr. Deborah Gilboa's books and insights on parenting Gen Z children.

Youth Mental Health:
http://www.ymhproject.org/
Randi Silverman and Wendy Ward co-founded The Youth Mental Health Project to help young parents and schools recognize early signs of mental health challenges in children. The organization was built around Randi's experience raising a child with bi-polar disorder. She created a full-length award-winning movie about her experience. Their passion and commitment to ending the stigma of teen mental health goes unmatched.

Teens and Generation Z - iGen:
www.jeantwenge.com
If you want or need to understand our youngest generation, Gen Z, you must read Dr. Jean Twenge's book, "iGen: Why Today's Super-Connected Kids Are Growing Up Less Rebellious, More Tolerant, Less Happy–and Completely Unprepared for Adulthood."

Marketing to Millennial Moms:
www.bsmmedia.com
If you want to reach Millennial Moms, Maria Bailey knows how. I highly encourage reading her book, "Millennial Moms; 202 Facts Marketers Need to Know to Build Brands and Drive Sales."

Volunteering and Philanthropy:
www.volunteermatch.org
Read: "Volunteer Engagement 2.0," introduced by Greg Baldwin, CEO VolunteerMatch. Follow him on LinkedIn and social media as well.

Helping Kids Reduce Their Screen Time
www.tomkersting.com

Read Tom Kersting's book, "Disconnected: How to Reconnect Our Digitally Distracted Kids." Follow his blog and attend one of his engaging speaking events to learn strategies to reduce your child's screen time.

Professional Development
www.blackrainpartners.com
A great organization that uses real-life business coaches who have walked the walk and talked the talk.

Writing a Book - Becoming an Author:
www.seandon.com
Read Sean Donovan's book, "The BookBook, a Recipe for Writing and Publishing Your Book." Sean has helped dozens of authors through his coaching, editing, and publishing consulting.

About

Dillon Kalkhurst

D. Knight Marketing & Consulting Group, Inc.

&

The Center for Intergenerational Engagement

Dillon Kalkhurst is an expert in Intergenerational Engagement. He has more than 25 years of experience in working with multi-generational families around the US education system. His specialty is creating broadcast media, community, and corporate alliances that support educational funding gaps. His ability to develop win-win-win partnerships that affect change and deliver positive social impact is unmatched.

Dillon is currently the Co-Founder and CMO (Chief Motivation Officer) at D. Knight Marketing & Consulting Group, a firm that helps corporations, school districts, and nonprofit organizations take advantage of their internal and external "Age Diversity." The firm helps create strategic partnerships that drive social impact and engage Millennials and Generation Z teens. Dillon also founded The Center for Intergenerational Engagement to support the findings in his book.

Dillon spent ten years as Director of Community Engagement and Strategic Partnerships at Scholastic. At Scholastic, Dillon engaged and motivated Scholastic's base of more than one million Millennial and Gen X parent and community volunteers. In his strategic partnership role, Dillon developed corporate, school, business, and community partnerships that raised over $10 million to support literacy projects for students in lower-income schools and districts.

One of the programs Dillon created and managed was "Read and Rise," a media and sponsor-supported campaign that provided books for underserved schools and communities. He developed alliances with more than 200 Clear Channel (now iHeart) radio stations that promoted the importance of independent reading. The "Read and Rise" Clear Channel Radio partnerships contributed over 100,000 books to kids in need. Dillon also represented Scholastic at national conferences and broadcast media appearances where he promoted Scholastic's mission of helping all children develop a love for reading.

Before joining Scholastic, Dillon was VP of Marketing and Partnership Development at Entertainment Publications, Inc. He created "One for the Community," an international campaign that partnered with more than 150 television stations, 65 professional sports teams, and hundreds of corporate supporters to raise awareness of school funding challenges while generating over $32 million in earned media to promote local education challenges and initiatives.

Dillon spent fifteen years in his early career in radio, starting in North Carolina where a close family friend owned and operated seven radio stations. He learned all aspects of the radio business by working in small to large markets. He continues to leverage his knowledge of the broadcasting industry to create win-win partnerships that benefit everyone involved. Dillon serves as an adviser and consultant for media companies, school districts, national nonprofit organizations, and youth family-targeted businesses, helping to grow their bottom line. He helps enhance company culture by teaching "Generational Harmony" and by crafting social impact campaigns that benefit their communities while meeting their business and organizational objectives.

Being an authority on "Intergenerational Engagement," Dillon is very active on social media and is a prolific and highly entertaining public speaker. As a professional photographer, he has perfected the art of storytelling by using images to demonstrate the impact of business, school, and community partnerships. Millions have viewed his social impact photographs and videos.

Dillon's companies, D. Knight Marketing and Consulting Group Inc, and The Center for Intergenerational Engagement help corporations embrace their Generational Diversity and coaches teams on how to master effective communication across generations. DKMC's specialties include: Intergenerational Engagement, Societal and Youth Marketing Campaigns, Non-Traditional/Cause Marketing Media Sales Campaigns, Sponsorship Sales, Strategic Partnership Development, Volunteer Engagement Initiatives, Event Production and Management, Video Production, Sales Training, and Motivational Speaking.

Dillon lives in the Orlando, FL metro area with his wife Linda and son Jordan, who is a junior in college studying to become a high school special education teacher.

Dillon Kalkhurst's Intergenerational Engagement team is always ready to help your organization improve communication and generational harmony.

Dillon is also available to speak at conventions, conferences, or sales training. This book, "GENERATION EVERYONE!" can be customized with a personalized greeting from your organizational leader or corporate sponsor. "GENERATION EVERYONE!" is a great follow-up gift for conference attendees.

If you would like to contact Mr. Kalkhurst to discuss your organization's Intergenerational Communications and Engagement needs, you can reach him here:

248

Dillon Kalkhurst
dillon@dknightmarketing.com
LinkedIn: linkedin.com/kalkhurst
Facebook: facebook.com/dillon.kalkhurst
Instagram: Instagram.com/kalkhurst

The Center for Intergenerational Engagement
www.5-gens.com

D. Knight Marketing and Consulting Group, Inc.
www.dknightmarketing.com

Made in the USA
Columbia, SC
24 March 2019